Welcome!

Thank you for joining us! This book powers our popular Data Structures and Algorithms online specialization on Coursera[1] and online MicroMasters program at edX[2]. See http://learningalgorithms.tilda.ws/ for more information about these online courses. We encourage you to sign up for a session and learn this material while interacting with thousands of other talented students from around the world. As you explore this book, you will find a number of active learning components that help you study the material at your own pace.

1. **PROGRAMMING CHALLENGES** ask you to implement the algorithms that you will encounter in one of programming languages that we support: C, C++, Java, JavaScript, Python, Scala, C#, Haskell, Ruby, and Rust (the last four programming languages are supported by Coursera only). These code challenges are embedded in our Coursera and edX online courses.

2. **ALGORITHMIC PUZZLES** provide you with a fun way to "invent" the key algorithmic ideas on your own! Even if you fail to solve some puzzles, the time will not be lost as you will better appreciate the beauty and power of algorithms. These puzzles are also embedded in our Coursera and edX online courses. We encourage you to try our puzzles before attempting to solve the programming challenges.

3. **EXERCISE BREAKS** offer "just in time" assessments testing your understanding of a topic before moving to the next one.

4. **STOP and THINK** questions invite you to slow down and contemplate the current material before continuing to the next topic.

[1] www.coursera.org/specializations/data-structures-algorithms
[2] www.edx.org/micromasters/ucsandiegox-algorithms-and-data-structures

Learning Algorithms Through Programming and Puzzle Solving

Alexander S. Kulikov and Pavel Pevzner

Active Learning Technologies

Printed in the United States of America

First Printing, 2018
ISBN: 978-0-9857312-1-2
Library of Congress Control Number: 2018907833

Active Learning Technologies

Address:
3520 Lebon Drive
Suite 5208
San Diego, CA 92122, USA

To my parents. — A.K.

To my family. — P.P.

vi

Contents

About This Book

I find that I don't understand things unless I try to program them.
—Donald E. Knuth, *The Art of Computer Programming*, Volume 4

There are many excellent books on Algorithms — why in the world we would write another one???

Because we feel that while these books excel in introducing algorithmic ideas, they have not yet succeeded in teaching you how to implement algorithms, the crucial computer science skill. Learning algorithms without implementing them is like learning surgery based solely on reading an anatomy book.

Our goal is to develop an *Intelligent Tutoring System* for learning algorithms through programming that can compete with the best professors in a traditional classroom. This *MOOC book* is the first step towards this goal written specifically for our Massive Open Online Courses (MOOCs) forming a specialization *"Algorithms and Data Structures"* on Coursera platform[3] and a microMasters program on edX platform[4]. Since the launch of our MOOCs in 2016, hundreds of thousand students enrolled in this specialization and tried to solve more than hundred algorithmic programming challenges to pass it. And some of them even got offers from small companies like Google after completing our specialization!

In the last few years, some professors expressed concerns about the pedagogical quality of MOOCs and even called them the "junk food of education." In contrast, we are among the growing group of professors who believe that traditional classes, that pack hundreds of students in a single classroom, represent junk food of education. In a large classroom, once a student takes a wrong turn, there are limited opportunities to ask a question, resulting in a *learning breakdown*, or the inability to progress further without individual guidance. Furthermore, the majority of time a student invests in an Algorithms course is spent completing assignments outside the classroom. That is why we stopped giving lectures in our offline classes (and we haven't got fired yet :-). Instead, we give *flipped classes* where students watch our recorded lectures, solve algorithmic puzzles, complete

---

[3]www.coursera.org/specializations/data-structures-algorithms
[4]www.edx.org/micromasters/ucsandiegox-algorithms-and-data-structures

programming challenges using our automated homework checking system before the class, and come to class prepared to discuss their learning breakdowns with us.

When a student suffers a learning breakdown, that student needs immediate help in order to proceed. Traditional textbooks do not provide such help, but our automated grading system described in this MOOC book does! Algorithms is a unique discipline in that students' ability to program provides the opportunity to automatically check their knowledge through coding challenges. These coding challenges are far superior to traditional quizzes that barely check whether a student fell asleep. Indeed, to implement a complex algorithm, the student must possess a deep understanding of its underlying algorithmic ideas.

We believe that a large portion of grading in thousands of Algorithms courses taught at various universities each year can be consolidated into a single automated system available at all universities. It did not escape our attention that many professors teaching algorithms have implemented their own custom-made systems for grading student programs, an illustration of academic inefficiency and lack of cooperation between various instructors. Our goal is to build a repository of algorithmic programming challenges, thus allowing professors to focus on teaching. We have already invested thousands of hours into building such a system and thousands students in our MOOCs tested it. Below we briefly describe how it works.

When you face a programming challenge, your goal is to implement a fast and memory-efficient algorithm for its solution. Solving programming challenges will help you better understand various algorithms and may even land you a job since many high-tech companies ask applicants to solve programming challenges during the interviews. Your implementation will be checked automatically against many carefully selected tests to verify that it always produces a correct answer and fits into the time and memory constrains. Our system will teach you to write programs that work correctly on all of our test datasets rather than on some of them. This is an important skill since failing to thoroughly test your programs leads to undetected bugs that frustrate your boss, your colleagues, and, most importantly, users of your programs.

You maybe wondering why it took thousands of hours to develop such a system. First, we had to build a Compendium of Learning Breakdowns for each programming challenge, 10–15 most frequent errors that students make while solving it. Afterwards, we had to develop test cases for each learning breakdown in each programming challenge, over 20 000 test cases for just 100 programming challenges in our specialization.

We encourage you to sign up for our *Algorithms and Data Structures* specialization on Coursera or MicroMasters program on edX and start interacting with thousands of talented students from around the world who are learning algorithms. Thank you for joining us!

Programming Challenges

This edition introduces basic algorithmic techniques using 30 programming challenges represented as icons below:

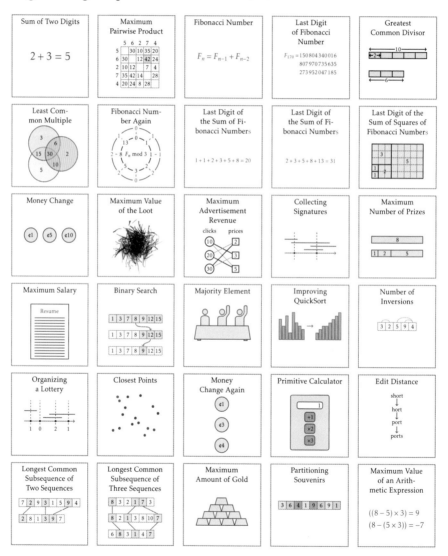

Interactive Algorithmic Puzzles

You are also welcome to solve the following interactive algorithmic puzzles available at http://dm.compsciclub.ru/app/list:

 Eight Queens. Place eight queens on the chessboard such that no two queens attack each other (a queen can move horizontally, vertically, or diagonally).

 Hanoi Towers. Move all disks from one peg to another using a minimum number of moves. In a single move, you can move a top disk from one peg to any other peg provided that you don't place a larger disk on the top of a smaller disk.

 Covering Segments by Points. Find the minimum number of points that cover all given segments on a line.

 Activity Selection. Select as many non-overlapping segments as possible.

 Largest Concatenate Problem. Compile the largest number by concatenating the given numbers.

 Black and White Squares. Use the minimum number of questions "What is the color of this square?" to find two neighboring squares of different colors. The leftmost square is white, the rightmost square is black, but the colors of all other squares are unknown.

 Twenty One Questions Game. Find an unknown integer $1 \le x \le N$ by asking the minimum number of questions "Is $x = y$?" (for any $1 \le y \le N$). Your opponent will reply either "Yes", or "$x < y$", or "$x > y$."

Book Sorting. Rearrange books on the shelf (in the increasing order of heights) using minimum number of swaps.

Number of Paths. Find out how many paths are there to get from the bottom left circle to any other circle and place this number inside the corresponding circle.

Antique Calculator. Find the minimum number of operations needed to get a positive integer n from the integer 1 using only three operations: add 1, multiply by 2, or multiply by 3.

Two Rocks Game. There are two piles of ten rocks. In each turn, you and your opponent may either take one rock from a single pile, or one rock from both piles. Your opponent moves first and the player that takes the last rock wins the game. Design a winning strategy.

Three Rocks Game. There are two piles of ten rocks. In each turn, you and your opponent may take up to three rocks. Your opponent moves first and the player that takes the last rock wins the game. Design a winning strategy.

Map Coloring. Use minimum number of colors such that neighboring countries are assigned different colors and each country is assigned a single color.

Clique Finding. Find the largest group of mutual friends (each pair of friends is represented by an edge).

Icosian Game. Find a cycle visiting each node exactly once.

Guarini Puzzle. Exchange the places of the white knights and the black knights. Two knights are not allowed to occupy the same cell of the chess board.

 Room Assignment. Place each student in one of her/his preferable rooms in a dormitory so that each room is occupied by a single student (preferable rooms are shown by edges).

 Tree Construction. Remove the minimum number of edges from the graph to make it acyclic.

 Subway Lines. You are planning a subway system where the subway lines should not cross. Can you connect each pair of the five stations except for a single pair?

What Lies Ahead

Watch for our future editions that will cover the following topics.

Data Structures

> Arrays and Lists
>
> Priority Queues
>
> Disjoint Sets
>
> Hash Tables
>
> Binary Search Trees

Algorithms on Graphs

> Graphs Decomposition
>
> Shortest Paths in Graphs
>
> Minimum Spanning Trees
>
> Shortest Paths in Real Life

Algorithms on Strings

> Pattern Matching
>
> Suffix Trees
>
> Suffix Arrays
>
> Burrows–Wheeler Transform

Advanced Algorithms and Complexity

> Flows in Networks
>
> Linear Programmings
>
> NP-complete Problems
>
> Coping with NP-completeness
>
> Streaming Algorithms

Meet the Authors

Alexander S. Kulikov is a senior research fellow at Steklov Mathematical Institute of the Russian Academy of Sciences, Saint Petersburg, Russia and a lecturer at the Department of Computer Science and Engineering at University of California, San Diego, USA. He also directs the Computer Science Center in Saint Petersburg that provides free advanced computer science courses complementing the standard university curricula. Alexander holds a Ph. D. from Steklov Mathematical Institute. His research interests include algorithms and complexity theory. He co-authored online courses "Data Structures and Algorithms" and "Introduction to Discrete Mathematics for Computer Science" that are available at Coursera and edX.

Pavel Pevzner is Ronald R. Taylor Professor of Computer Science at the University of California, San Diego. He holds a Ph. D. from Moscow Institute of Physics and Technology, Russia and an Honorary Degree from Simon Fraser University. He is a Howard Hughes Medical Institute Professor (2006), an Association for Computing Machinery Fellow (2010), an International Society for Computational Biology Fellow (2012), and a Member of the the Academia Europaea (2016). He has authored the textbooks Computational Molecular Biology: An Algorithmic Approach (2000), An Introduction to Bioinformatics Algorithms (2004) (jointly with Neil Jones), and Bioinformatics Algorithms: An Active Learning Approach (2014) (jointly with Phillip Compeau). He co-authored online courses "Data Structures and Algorithms", "Bioinformatics", and "Analyze Your Genome!" that are available at Coursera and edX.

Meet Our Online Co-Instructors

 **Daniel Kane** is an associate professor at the University of California, San Diego with a joint appointment between the Department of Computer Science and Engineering and the Department of Mathematics. He has diverse interests in mathematics and theoretical computer science, though most of his work fits into the broad categories of number theory, complexity theory, or combinatorics.

 **Michael Levin** is an Associate Professor at the Computer Science Department of Higher School of Economics, Moscow, Russia and the Chief Data Scientist at the Yandex.Market, Moscow, Russia. He also teaches Algorithms and Data Structures at the Yandex School of Data Analysis.

 **Neil Rhodes** is a lecturer in the Computer Science and Engineering department at the University of California, San Diego and formerly a staff software engineer at Google. Neil holds a B.A. and M.S. in Computer Science from UCSD. He left the Ph.D. program at UCSD to start a company, Palomar Software, and spent fifteen years writing software, books on software development, and designing and teaching programming courses for Apple and Palm. He's taught Algorithms, Machine Learning, Operating Systems, Discrete Mathematics, Automata and Computability Theory, and Software Engineering at UCSD and Harvey Mudd College in Claremont, California.

Acknowledgments

This book was greatly improved by the efforts of a large number of individuals, to whom we owe a debt of gratitude.

Our co-instructors and partners in crime Daniel Kane, Michael Levin, and Neil Rhodes invested countless hours in the development of our online courses at Coursera and edX platforms.

Hundreds of thousands of our online students provided valuable feedback that led to many improvements in our MOOCs and this MOOC book. In particular, we are grateful to the mentors of the Algorithmic Toolbox class at Coursera: Ayoub Falah, Denys Diachenko, Kishaan Jeeveswaran, Irina Pinjaeva, Fernando Gonzales Vigil Richter, and Gabrio Secco.

We thank our colleagues who helped us with preparing programming challenges: Maxim Akhmedov, Roman Andreev, Gleb Evstropov, Nikolai Karpov, Sergey Poromov, Sergey Kopeliovich, Ilya Kornakov, Gennady Korotkevich, Paul Melnichuk, and Alexander Tiunov.

We are grateful to Anton Konev for leading the development of interactive puzzles as well as Anton Belyaev and Kirill Banaru for help with some of the puzzles.

We thank Alexey Kladov, Sergey Lebedev, Alexei Levin, Sergey Shulman, and Alexander Smal for help with the "Good Programming Practices" section of the book.

Randall Christopher brought to life our idea for the textbook cover.

Finally, our families helped us preserve our sanity when we were working on this MOOC book.

A. K. and P. P.
Saint Petersburg and San Diego
December 2017

Chapter 1: Algorithms and Complexity

This book presents programming challenges that will teach you how to design and implement algorithms. Solving a programming challenge is one of the best ways to understand an algorithm's design as well as to identify its potential weaknesses and fix them.

1.1   What Is an Algorithm?

Roughly speaking, an algorithm is a sequence of instructions that one must perform in order to solve a well-formulated problem. We will specify problems in terms of their *inputs* and their *outputs*, and the algorithm will be the method of translating the inputs into the outputs. A well-formulated problem is unambiguous and precise, leaving no room for misinterpretation.

After you designed an algorithm, two important questions to ask are: "Does it work correctly?" and "How much time will it take?" Certainly you would not be satisfied with an algorithm that only returned correct results half the time, or took 1000 years to arrive at an answer.

1.2   Pseudocode

To understand how an algorithm works, we need some way of listing the steps that the algorithm takes, while being neither too vague nor too formal. We will use *pseudocode*, a language computer scientists often use to describe algorithms. Pseudocode ignores many of the details that are required in a programming language, yet it is more precise and less ambiguous than, say, a recipe in a cookbook.

1.3   Problem Versus Problem Instance

A problem describes a class of computational tasks. A problem instance is one particular input from that class. To illustrate the difference between a problem and an instance of a problem, consider the following example. You find yourself in a bookstore buying a book for $4.23 which you pay for with a \$5 bill. You would be due 77 cents in change, and the cashier now makes a decision as to exactly how you get it. You would be annoyed at a fistful of 77 pennies or 15 nickels and 2 pennies, which raises the question of how to make change in the least annoying way. Most cashiers try to minimize the number of coins returned for a particular quantity of change. The example of 77 cents represents an instance of the Change Problem, which we describe below.

The example of 77 cents represents an instance of the Change Problem that assumes that there are d denominations represented by an array $c = (c_1, c_2, \ldots, c_d)$. For simplicity, we assume that the denominations are given in decreasing order of value. For example, $c = (25, 10, 5, 1)$ for United States denominations.

Change Problem

Convert some amount of money into given denominations, using the smallest possible number of coins.

> **Input:** An integer *money* and an array of d denominations $c = (c_1, c_2, \ldots, c_d)$, in decreasing order of value ($c_1 > c_2 > \cdots > c_d$).
> **Output:** A list of d integers $i_1, i_2, \ldots, i_d$ such that $c_1 \cdot i_1 + c_2 \cdot i_2 + \cdots + c_d \cdot i_d = money$, and $i_1 + i_2 + \cdots + i_d$ is as small as possible.

The algorithm that is used by cashiers all over the world to solve this problem is simple:

CHANGE(*money*, *c*, *d*):
while *money* > 0:
  coin ← coin with the largest denomination that does not exceed *money*
  give coin with denomination *coin* to customer
  money ← *money* − *coin*

Here is a faster version of CHANGE:

CHANGE(*money*, *c*, *d*):
r ← *money*
for k from 1 to d:
  $i_k \leftarrow \lfloor \frac{r}{c_k} \rfloor$
  $r \leftarrow r - c_k \cdot i_k$
return $(i_1, i_2, \ldots, i_d)$

1.4 Correct Versus Incorrect Algorithms

We say that an algorithm is correct when it translates every input instance into the correct output. An algorithm is incorrect when there is at least one input instance for which the algorithm gives an incorrect output.

CHANGE is an incorrect algorithm! Suppose you were changing 40 cents into coins with denominations of $c_1 = 25$, $c_2 = 20$, $c_3 = 10$, $c_4 = 5$, and $c_5 = 1$. CHANGE would incorrectly return 1 quarter, 1 dime, and 1 nickel, instead of 2 twenty-cent pieces. As contrived as this may seem, in 1875 a twenty-cent coin existed in the United States. How sure can we be that CHANGE returns the minimal number of coins for the modern US denominations or for denominations in any other country?

To correct the CHANGE algorithm, we could consider every possible combination of coins with denominations $c_1, c_2, \ldots, c_d$ that adds to *money*, and return the combination with the fewest. We only need to consider combinations with $i_1 \leq money/c_1$ and $i_2 \leq money/c_2$ (in general, i_k should not exceed $money/c_k$), because we would otherwise be returning an amount of money larger than *money*. The pseudocode below uses the symbol $\sum$ that stands for summation: $\sum_{i=1}^{m} a_i = a_1 + a_2 + \cdots + a_m$. The pseudocode also uses the notion of "infinity" (denoted as ∞) as an initial value for *smallestNumberOfCoins*; there are a number of ways to carry this out in a real computer, but the details are not important here.

```
BRUTEFORCECHANGE(money, c, d):
smallestNumberOfCoins ← ∞
for each (i_1,...,i_d) from (0,...,0) to (money/c_1,..., money/c_d)
    valueOfCoins ← ∑_{k=1}^{d} i_k · c_k
    if valueOfCoins = M:
        numberOfCoins = ∑_{k=1}^{d} i_k
        if numberOfCoins < smallestNumberOfCoins:
            smallestNumberOfCoins ← numberOfCoins
            change ← (i_1, i_2,..., i_d)
return change
```

The second line iterates over every feasible combination $(i_1, \ldots, i_d)$ of the d indices, and stops when it has reached $(money/c_1, \ldots, money/c_d)$.

How do we know that BRUTEFORCECHANGE does not suffer from the same problem as CHANGE did, namely that it generates incorrect result for some input instance?? Since BruteForceChange explores all feasible combinations of denominations, it will eventually come across an optimal solution and record it as such in the *change* array. Any combination of coins that adds to M must have at least as many coins as the optimal combination, so BruteForceChange will never overwrite *change* with a suboptimal solution.

So far we have answered only one of the two important algorithmic questions ("Does it work?", but not "How much time will it take?").

Stop and Think. How fast is BruteForceChange?

1.5　Fast Versus Slow Algorithms

Real computers require a certain amount of time to perform an operation such as addition, subtraction, or testing the conditions in a while loop. A supercomputer might take 10^{-10} second to perform an addition, while a calculator might take 10^{-5} second. Suppose that you had a computer that took 10^{-10} second to perform an elementary operation such as addition, and that you knew how many operations a particular algorithm would perform. You could estimate the running time of the algorithm simply by taking the product of the number of operations and the time per operation. However, computers are constantly improving, leading to a decreasing time per operation, so your notion of the running time would soon be outdated. Rather than computing an algorithm's running time on every computer, we rely on the total number of operations that the algorithm performs to describe its running time, since this is an attribute of the algorithm, and not an attribute of the computer you happen to be using.

Unfortunately, determining how many operations an algorithm will perform is not always easy. If we know how to compute the number of basic operations that an algorithm performs, then we have a basis to compare it against a different algorithm that solves the same problem. Rather than tediously count every multiplication and addition, we can perform this comparison by gaining a high-level understanding of the growth of each algorithm's operation count as the size of the input increases.

Suppose an algorithm A performs $11n^3$ operations on an input of size n, and an algorithm B solves the same problem in $99n^2 + 7$ operations. Which algorithm, A or B, is faster? Although A may be faster than B for some small n (e.g., for n between 0 and 9), B will become faster for large n (e.g., for all $n > 10$). Since n^3 is, in some sense, a "faster-growing" function than n^2 with respect to n, the constants 11, 99, and 7 do not affect the competition between the two algorithms for large n. We refer to A as a *cubic* algorithm and to B as a *quadratic* algorithm, and say that A is less efficient than B because it performs more operations to solve the same problem when n is large. Thus, we will often be somewhat imprecise when we count operations of an algorithm—the behavior of algorithms on small inputs does not matter.

Let's estimate the number of operations BRUTEFORCECHANGE will take on an input instance of M cents, and denominations $(c_1, c_2, \ldots, c_d)$. To calculate the total number of operations in the for loop, we can take the approximate number of operations performed in each iteration and multiply this by the total number of iterations. Since there are roughly

$$\frac{money}{c_1} \times \frac{money}{c_2} \times \cdots \times \frac{money}{c_d}$$

iterations, the for loop performs on the order of $d \times \frac{money^d}{c_1 c_2 \cdots c_d}$ operations, which dwarfs the other operations of the algorithm.

This type of algorithm is often referred to as an *exponential* algorithm in contrast to quadratic, cubic, or other *polynomial* algorithms. The expression for the running time of exponential algorithms includes a term like n^d, where n and d are parameters of the problem (i.e., n and d may deliberately be made arbitrarily large by changing the input to the algorithm), while the running time of a polynomial algorithm is bounded by a term like n^k where k is a constant not related to the size of any parameters.

For example, an algorithm with running time n^1 (linear), n^2 (quadratic), n^3 (cubic), or even n^{2018} is polynomial. Of course, an algorithm with running time n^{2018} is not very practical, perhaps less so than some exponential algorithms, and much effort in computer science goes into designing faster and faster polynomial algorithms. Since d may be large when the algorithm is called with a long list of denominations (e.g., $c = (1, 2, 3, 4, 5, \ldots, 100)$), we see that BRUTEFORCECHANGE can take a very long time to execute.

1.6   Big-O Notation

Computer scientists use the *Big-O notation* to describe concisely the running time of an algorithm. If we say that the running time of an algorithm is quadratic, or $O(n^2)$, it means that the running time of the algorithm on an input of size n is limited by a quadratic function of n. That limit may be $99.7n^2$ or $0.001n^2$ or $5n^2 + 3.2n + 99993$; the main factor that describes the growth rate of the running time is the term that grows the fastest with respect to n, for example n^2 when compared to terms like $3.2n$, or 99993. All functions with a leading term of n^2 have more or less the same rate of growth, so we lump them into one class which we call $O(n^2)$. The difference in behavior between two quadratic functions in that class, say $99.7n^2$ and $5n^2 + 3.2n + 99993$, is negligible when compared to the difference in behavior between two functions in different classes, say $5n^2 + 3.2n$ and $1.2n^3$. Of course, $99.7n^2$ and $5n^2$ are different functions and we would prefer an algorithm that takes $5n^2$ operations to an algorithm that takes $99.7n^2$. However, computer scientists typically ignore the leading constant and pay attention only to the fastest growing term.

When we write $f(n) = O(n^2)$, we mean that the function $f(n)$ does not grow faster than a function with a leading term of cn^2, for a suitable choice of the constant c. In keeping with the healthy dose of pessimism toward an algorithm's performance, we measure an algorithm's efficiency as its worst case efficiency, which is the largest amount of time an algorithm can take given the worst possible input of a given size. The advantage to considering the worst case efficiency of an algorithm is that we are guaranteed that our algorithm will never behave worse than our worst case estimate, so we are never surprised or disappointed. Thus, when we derive a Big-O bound, it is a bound on the worst case efficiency.

Chapter 2: Algorithm Design Techniques

Over the last half a century, computer scientists have discovered that many algorithms share similar ideas, even though they solve very different problems. There appear to be relatively few basic techniques that can be applied when designing an algorithm, and we cover some of them later in various programming challenges in this book. For now we will mention the most common algorithm design techniques, so that future examples can be categorized in terms of the algorithm's design methodology.

To illustrate the design techniques, we will consider a very simple problem that plagued nearly everyone before the era of mobile phones when people used cordless phones. Suppose your cordless phone rings, but you have misplaced the handset somewhere in your home. How do you find it? To complicate matters, you have just walked into your home with an armful of groceries, and it is dark out, so you cannot rely solely on eyesight.

2.1 Exhaustive Search Algorithms

An *exhaustive search*, or *brute force*, algorithm examines every possible alternative to find one particular solution. For example, if you used the brute force algorithm to find the ringing telephone, you would ignore the ringing of the phone, as if you could not hear it, and simply walk over every square inch of your home checking to see if the phone was present. You probably would not be able to answer the phone before it stopped ringing, unless you were very lucky, but you would be guaranteed to eventually find the phone no matter where it was.

BRUTEFORCECHANGE is a brute force algorithm, and our programming challenges include some additional examples of such algorithms—these are the easiest algorithms to design, and sometimes they work for certain practical problems. In general, though, brute force algorithms are too slow to be practical for anything but the smallest instances and you should always think how to avoid the brute force algorithms or how to finesse them into faster versions.

2.2   Branch-and-Bound Algorithms

In certain cases, as we explore the various alternatives in a brute force algorithm, we discover that we can omit a large number of alternatives, a technique that is often called *branch-and-bound*.

Suppose you were exhaustively searching the first floor and heard the phone ringing above your head. You could immediately rule out the need to search the basement or the first floor. What may have taken three hours may now only take one, depending on the amount of space that you can rule out.

2.3   Greedy Algorithms

Many algorithms are iterative procedures that choose among a number of alternatives at each iteration. For example, a cashier can view the Change Problem as a series of decisions he or she has to make: which coin (among d denominations) to return first, which to return second, and so on. Some of these alternatives may lead to correct solutions while others may not.

Greedy algorithms choose the "most attractive" alternative at each iteration, for example, the largest denomination possible. In the case of the US denominations, CHANGE used quarters, then dimes, then nickels, and finally pennies (in that order) to make change. Of course, we showed that this greedy strategy produced incorrect results when certain new denominations were included.

In the telephone example, the corresponding greedy algorithm would simply be to walk in the direction of the telephone's ringing until you found it. The problem here is that there may be a wall (or a fragile vase) between you and the phone, preventing you from finding it. Unfortunately, these sorts of difficulties frequently occur in most realistic problems. In many cases, a greedy approach will seem "obvious" and natural, but will be subtly wrong.

2.4   Dynamic Programming Algorithms

Some algorithms break a problem into smaller subproblems and use the solutions of the subproblems to construct the solution of the larger one.

During this process, the number of subproblems may become very large, and some algorithms solve the same subproblem repeatedly, needlessly increasing the running time. Dynamic programming organizes computations to avoid recomputing values that you already know, which can often save a great deal of time.

The Ringing Telephone Problem does not lend itself to a dynamic programming solution, so we consider a different problem to illustrate the technique. Suppose that instead of answering the phone you decide to play the "Rocks" game with two piles of rocks, say ten in each. In each turn, one player may take either one rock (from either pile) or two rocks (one from each pile). Once the rocks are taken, they are removed from play. The player that takes the last rock wins the game. You make the first move. We encourage you to play this game using our interactive puzzle.

To find the winning strategy for the 10+10 game, we can construct a table, which we can call R, shown in Figure 2.1. Instead of solving a problem with 10 rocks in each pile, we will solve a more general problem with n rocks in one pile and m rocks in the other pile (the $n + m$ game) where n and m are arbitrary non-negative integers.

If Player 1 can always win the $n + m$ game, then we would say $R(n, m) = W$, but if Player 1 has no winning strategy against a player that always makes the right moves, we would write $R(n, m) = L$. Computing $R(n, m)$ for arbitrary n and m seems difficult, but we can build on smaller values. Some games, notably $R(0, 1)$, $R(1, 0)$, and $R(1, 1)$, are clearly winning propositions for Player 1 since in the first move, Player 1 can win. Thus, we fill in entries $(1, 1)$, $(0, 1)$, and $(1, 0)$ as W. See Figure 2.1(a).

After the entries $(0, 1)$, $(1, 0)$, and $(1, 1)$ are filled, one can try to fill other entries. For example, in the $(2, 0)$ case, the only move that Player 1 can make leads to the $(1, 0)$ case that, as we already know, is a winning position for his opponent. A similar analysis applies to the $(0, 2)$ case, leading to the table in Figure 2.1(b).

In the $(2, 1)$ case, Player 1 can make three different moves that lead respectively to the games of $(1, 1)$, $(2, 0)$, or $(1, 0)$. One of these cases, $(2, 0)$, leads to a losing position for his opponent and therefore $(2, 1)$ is a winning position. The case $(1, 2)$ is symmetric to $(2, 1)$, so we have the table shown at Figure 2.1(c).

Now we can fill in $R(2, 2)$. In the $(2, 2)$ case, Player 1 can make three different moves that lead to entries $(2, 1)$, $(1, 2)$, and $(1, 1)$. All of these entries are winning positions for his opponent and therefore $R(2, 2) = L$,

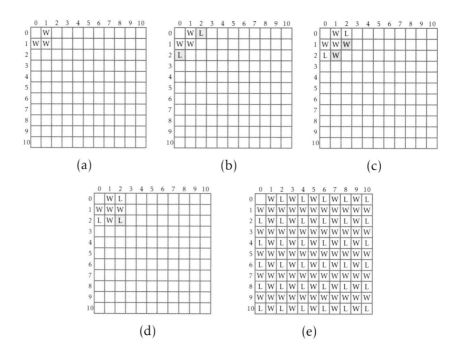

Figure 2.1: Table R for the $10+10$ Rocks game.

see Figure 2.1(d).

We can proceed filling in R in this way by noticing that for the entry (i, j) to be L, the entries above, diagonally to the left, and directly to the left, must be W. These entries ($(i-1, j)$, $(i-1, j-1)$, and $(i, j-1)$) correspond to the three possible moves that Player 1 can make. See Figure 2.1(e).

The ROCKS algorithm determines if Player 1 wins or loses. If Player 1 wins in an $n+m$ game, ROCKS returns W. If Player 1 loses, ROCKS returns L. We introduced an artificial initial condition, $R(0, 0) = L$ to simplify the pseudocode.

```
ROCKS(n, m):
R(0, 0) ← L
for i from 1 to n:
    if R(i − 1, 0) = W:
        R(i, 0) ← L
    else:
        R(i, 0) ← W
for j from 1 to m:
    if R(0, j − 1) = W:
        R(0, j) ← L
    else:
        R(0, j) ← W
for i from 1 to n:
    for j from 1 to m:
        if R(i − 1, j − 1) = W and R(i, j − 1) = W and R(i − 1, j) = W:
            R(i, j) ← L
        else:
            R(i, j) ← W
return R(n, m)
```

A faster algorithm to solve the Rocks puzzle relies on the simple pattern in R, and checks if n and m are both even, in which case the player loses (see table above).

```
FASTROCKS(n, m):
if n and m are both even:
    return L
else:
    return W
```

However, though FastRocks is more efficient than Rocks, it may be difficult to modify it for similar games, for example, a game in which each player can move up to three rocks at a time from the piles. This is one example where the slower algorithm is more instructive than a faster one.

Exercise Break. Play the Three Rocks game using our interactive puzzle and construct the dynamic programming table similar to the table above for this game.

2.5   Recursive Algorithms

Recursion is one of the most ubiquitous algorithmic concepts. Simply, an algorithm is recursive if it calls itself.

The *Towers of Hanoi puzzle* consists of three pegs, which we label from left to right as 1, 2, and 3, and a number of disks of decreasing radius, each with a hole in the center. The disks are initially stacked on the left peg (peg 1) so that smaller disks are on top of larger ones. The game is played by moving one disk at a time between pegs. You are only allowed to place smaller disks on top of larger ones, and any disk may go onto an empty peg. The puzzle is solved when all of the disks have been moved from peg 1 to peg 3. Try our interactive puzzle Hanoi Towers to figure out how to move all disks from one peg to another.

Towers of Hanoi Problem
Output a list of moves that solves the Towers of Hanoi.

> **Input:** An integer n.
> **Output:** A sequence of moves that solve the n-disk Towers of Hanoi puzzle.

Solving the puzzle with one disk is easy: move the disk to the right peg. The two-disk puzzle is not much harder: move the small disk to the middle peg, then the large disk to the right peg, then the small disk to the right peg to rest on top of the large disk.

The three-disk puzzle is somewhat harder, but the following sequence of seven moves solves it:

1. Move disk from peg 1 to peg 3

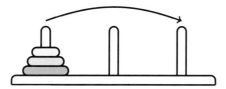

2. Move disk from peg 1 to peg 2

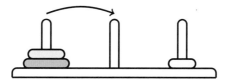

3. Move disk from peg 3 to peg 2

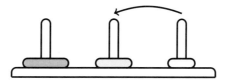

4. Move disk from peg 1 to peg 3

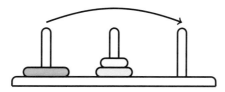

5. Move disk from peg 2 to peg 1

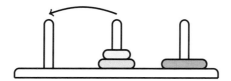

6. Move disk from peg 2 to peg 3

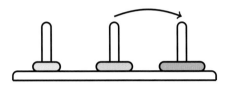

7. Move disk from peg 1 to peg 3

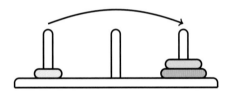

Now we will figure out how many steps are required to solve a four-disk puzzle. You cannot complete this game without moving the largest disk. However, in order to move the largest disk, we first had to move all the smaller disks to an empty peg. If we had four disks instead of three, then we would first have to move the top three to an empty peg (7 moves), then move the largest disk (1 move), then again move the three disks from their temporary peg to rest on top of the largest disk (another 7 moves). The whole procedure will take $7 + 1 + 7 = 15$ moves.

More generally, to move a stack of size n from the left to the right peg, you first need to move a stack of size $n-1$ from the left to the middle peg, and then from the middle peg to the right peg once you have moved the n-th disk to the right peg. To move a stack of size $n-1$ from the middle to the right, you first need to move a stack of size $n-2$ from the middle to the left, then move the $(n-1)$-th disk to the right, and then move the stack of size $n-2$ from the left to the right peg, and so on.

At first glance, the Towers of Hanoi Problem looks difficult. However, the following *recursive algorithm* solves the Towers of Hanoi Problem with just 9 lines!

HanoiTowers($n, fromPeg, toPeg$)
if $n = 1$:
   output "Move disk from peg *fromPeg* to peg *toPeg*"
   return
unusedPeg ← 6 − *fromPeg* − *toPeg*
HanoiTowers($n − 1, fromPeg, unusedPeg$)
output "Move disk from peg *fromPeg* to peg *toPeg*"
HanoiTowers($n − 1, unusedPeg, toPeg$)
return

The variables *fromPeg*, *toPeg*, and *unusedPeg* refer to the three differ-ent pegs so that HanoiTowers($n, 1, 3$) moves n disks from the first peg to the third peg. The variable *unusedPeg* represents which of the three pegs can serve as a temporary destination for the first $n − 1$ disks. Note that *fromPeg* + *toPeg* + *unusedPeg* is always equal to $1 + 2 + 3 = 6$, so the value of the variable *unusedPeg* can be computed as $6 − fromPeg − toPeg$. Table below shows the result of $6 − fromPeg − toPeg$ for all possible values of *fromPeg* and *toPeg*.

fromPeg	toPeg	unusedPeg
1	2	3
1	3	2
2	1	3
2	3	1
3	1	2
3	2	1

After computing *unusedPeg* as $6 − fromPeg − toPeg$, the statements

HanoiTowers($n − 1, fromPeg, unusedPeg$)
output "Move disk from peg *fromPeg* to peg *toPeg*"
HanoiTowers($n − 1, unusedPeg, toPeg$)
return

solve the smaller problem of moving the stack of size $n − 1$ first to the temporary space, moving the largest disk, and then moving the $n − 1$ re-maining disks to the final destination. Note that we do not have to specify which disk the player should move from *fromPeg* to *toPeg*: it is always the top disk currently residing on *fromPeg* that gets moved.

Although the Hanoi Tower solution can be expressed in just 9 lines of pseudocode, it requires a surprisingly long time to run. To solve a five-disk tower requires 31 moves, but to solve a hundred-disk tower would require more moves than there are atoms on Earth. The fast growth of the number of moves that HANOITOWERS requires is easy to see by noticing that every time HANOITOWERS($n, 1, 3$) is called, it calls itself twice for $n - 1$, which in turn triggers four calls for $n - 2$, and so on.

We can illustrate this situation in a *recursion tree*, which is shown in Figure 2.2. A call to HANOITOWERS($4, 1, 3$) results in calls HANOITOWERS($3, 1, 2$) and HANOITOWERS($3, 2, 3$); each of these results in calls to HANOITOWERS($2, 1, 3$), HANOITOWERS($2, 3, 2$) and HANOITOWERS($2, 2, 1$), HANOITOWERS($2, 1, 3$), and so on. Each call to the subroutine HANOITOWERS requires some amount of time, so we would like to know how much time the algorithm will take.

To calculate the running time of HANOITOWERS of size n, we denote the number of disk moves that HANOITOWERS(n) performs as $T(n)$ and notice that the following equation holds:

$$T(n) = 2 \cdot T(n - 1) + 1 .$$

Starting from $T(1) = 1$, this recurrence relation produces the sequence:

$$1, 3, 7, 15, 31, 63,$$

and so on. We can compute $T(n)$ by adding 1 to both sides and noticing

$$T(n) + 1 = 2 \cdot T(n - 1) + 1 + 1 = 2 \cdot (T(n - 1) + 1).$$

If we introduce a new variable, $U(n) = T(n) + 1$, then $U(n) = 2 \cdot U(n - 1)$. Thus, we have changed the problem to the following recurrence relation.

$$U(n) = 2 \cdot U(n - 1).$$

Starting from $U(1) = 2$, this gives rise to the sequence

$$2, 4, 8, 16, 32, 64, \ldots$$

implying that at $U(n) = 2^n$ and $T(n) = U(n) - 1 = 2^n - 1$. Thus, HANOITOWERS($n$) is an exponential algorithm.

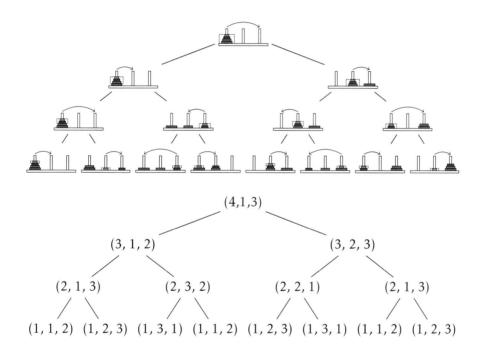

Figure 2.2: The recursion tree for a call to HANOITOWERS(4, 1, 3), which solves the Towers of Hanoi problem of size 4. At each point in the tree, (i, j, k) stands for HANOITOWERS(i, j, k).

2.6 Divide-and-Conquer Algorithms

One big problem may be hard to solve, but two problems that are half the size may be significantly easier. In these cases, divide-and-conquer algorithms fare well by doing just that: splitting the problem into smaller subproblems, solving the subproblems independently, and combining the solutions of subproblems into a solution of the original problem. The situation is usually more complicated than this and after splitting one problem into subproblems, a divide-and-conquer algorithm usually splits these subproblems into even smaller sub-subproblems, and so on, until it reaches a point at which it no longer needs to recurse. A critical step in many divide-and-conquer algorithms is the recombining of solutions to subproblems into a solution for a larger problem.

To give an example of a divide-and conquer algorithm, we will consider the sorting problem:

Sorting Problem
Sort a list of integers.

Input: A list of n distinct integers $a = (a_1, a_2, \ldots, a_n)$.
Output: Sorted list of integers, that is, a reordering $b = (b_1, b_2, \ldots, b_n)$ of integers from a such that $b_1 < b_2 < \cdots < b_n$.

SELECTIONSORT is a simple iterative method to solve the Sorting Problem. It first finds the smallest element in a, and moves it to the first position by swapping it with whatever happens to be in the first position (i.e., a_1). Next, it finds the second smallest element in a, and moves it to the second position, again by swapping with a_2 . At the i-th iteration, SELECTIONSORT finds the i-th smallest element in a, and moves it to the i-th position. This is an intuitive approach at sorting, but is not the fastest one.

If $a = (7, 92, 87, 1, 4, 3, 2, 6)$, SELECTIONSORT$(a, 8)$ takes the following seven steps:

$$(7, 92, 87, 1, 4, 3, 2, 6)$$
$$(1, 92, 87, 7, 4, 3, 2, 6)$$
$$(1, 2, 87, 7, 4, 3, 92, 6)$$
$$(1, 2, 3, 7, 4, 87, 92, 6)$$

$$(1, 2, 3, 4, 7, 87, 92, 6)$$
$$(1, 2, 3, 4, 6, 87, 92, 7)$$
$$(1, 2, 3, 4, 6, 7, 92, 87)$$
$$(1, 2, 3, 4, 6, 7, 87, 92)$$

MERGESORT is a canonical example of divide-and-conquer sorting algorithm that is much faster than SELECTIONSORT. We begin from the problem of *merging*, in which we want to combine two sorted lists $List_1$ and $List_2$ into a single sorted list.

$List_1$	2 5 7 8 |	2 5 7 8 |	2 5 7 8 |	2 5 7 8 |	2 5 7 8 |	2 5 7 8
$List_2$	3 4 6 |	3 4 6 |	3 4 6 |	3 4 6 |	3 4 6 |	3 4 6
sortedList	2	3	4	5	6	7 8

The MERGE algorithm combines two sorted lists into a single sorted list in $O(|List_1| + |List_2|)$ time by iteratively choosing the smallest remaining element in $List_1$ and $List_2$ and moving it to the growing sorted list.

MERGE($List_1, List_2$):
$SortedList \leftarrow$ empty list
while both $List_1$ and $List_2$ are non-empty:
    if the smallest element in $List_1$ is smaller than the smallest element in $List_2$
        move the smallest element from $List_1$ to the end of $SortedList$
    else:
        move the smallest element from $List_2$ to the end of $SortedList$
move any remaining elements from either $List_1$ or $List_2$ to the end of $SortedList$
return $SortedList$

MERGE would be useful for sorting an arbitrary list if we knew how to divide an arbitrary (unsorted) list into two already sorted half-sized lists. However, it may seem that we are back to where we started, except now we have to sort two smaller lists instead of one big one. Yet sorting two smaller lists is a preferable algorithmic problem. To see why, let's consider the MERGESORT algorithm, which divides an unsorted list into two parts and then recursively conquers each smaller sorting problem before merging the sorted lists.

MERGESORT(*List*):
if *List* consists of a single element:
    return *List*
FirstHalf ← first half of *List*
SecondHalf ← second half of *List*
SortedFirstHalf ← MERGESORT(*FirstHalf*)
SortedSecondHalf ← MERGESORT(*SecondHalf*)
SortedList ← MERGE(*SortedFirstHalf*, *SortedSecondHalf*)
return *SortedList*

Stop and Think. What is the runtime of MERGESORT?

Figure 2.3 shows the recursion tree of MERGESORT, consisting of $\log_2 n$ levels, where n is the size of the original unsorted list. At the bottom level, we must merge two sorted lists of approximately $n/2$ elements each, requiring $O(n/2 + n/2) = O(n)$ time. At the next highest level, we must merge four lists of $n/4$ elements, requiring $O(n/4 + n/4 + n/4 + n/4) = O(n)$ time. This pattern can be generalized: the i-th level contains 2^i lists, each having approximately $n/2^i$ elements, and requires $O(n)$ time to merge. Since there are $\log_2 n$ levels in the recursion tree, MERGESORT requires $O(n \log_2 n)$ runtime overall, which offers a speedup over a naive $O(n^2)$ sorting algorithm.

2.7 Randomized Algorithms

If you happen to have a coin, then before even starting to search for the phone, you could toss it to decide whether you want to start your search on the first floor if the coin comes up heads, or on the second floor if the coin comes up tails. If you also happen to have a die, then after deciding on the second floor of your mansion, you could roll it to decide in which of the six rooms on the second floor to start your search. Although tossing coins and rolling dice may be a fun way to search for the phone, it is certainly not the intuitive thing to do, nor is it at all clear whether it gives you any algorithmic advantage over a deterministic algorithm. Our programming challenges will help you to learn why randomized algorithms are useful and why some of them have a competitive advantage over deterministic algorithms.

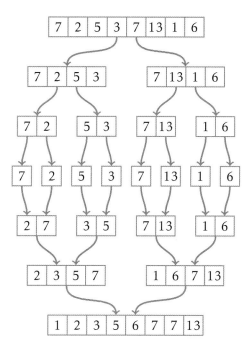

Figure 2.3:   The recursion tree for sorting an 8-element array with
MERGESORT. The divide (upper) steps consist of $\log_2 8 = 3$ levels, where
the input array is split into smaller and smaller subarrays. The conquer
(lower) steps consist of the same number of levels, as the sorted subarrays
are merged back together.

To give an example of a randomized algorithm, we will first discuss a fast sorting technique called QUICKSORT. It selects an element m (typically, the first) from an array c and simply partitions the array into two subarrays: c_{small}, containing all elements from c that are smaller than m; and c_{large} containing all elements larger than m.

This partitioning can be done in linear time, and by following a divide-and-conquer strategy, QUICKSORT recursively sorts each subarray in the same way. The sorted list is easily created by simply concatenating the sorted c_{small}, element m, and the sorted c_{large}.

QUICKSORT(c):
if c consists of a single element:
    return c
$m \leftarrow c[1]$
determine the set of elements c_{small} smaller than m
determine the set of elements c_{large} larger than m
QUICKSORT(c_{small})
QUICKSORT(c_{large})
combine c_{small}, m, and c_{large} into a single sorted array c_{sorted}
return c_{sorted}

It turns out that the running time of QUICKSORT depends on how lucky we are with our selection of the element m. If we happen to choose m in such a way that the array c is split into even halves (i.e., $|c_{small}| = |c_{large}|$), then

$$T(n) = 2T\left(\frac{n}{2}\right) + a \cdot n,$$

where $T(n)$ represents the time taken by QUICKSORT to sort an array of n numbers, and $a \cdot n$ represents the time required to split the array of size n into two parts; a is a positive constant. This is exactly the same recurrence as in MERGESORT that leads to $O(n \log n)$ running time.

However, if we choose m in such a way that it splits c unevenly (e.g., an extreme case occurs when c_{small} is empty and c_{large} has $n-1$ elements), then the recurrence looks like

$$T(n) = T(n-1) + a \cdot n.$$

This is the recurrence that leads to $O(n^2)$ running time, something we want to avoid. Indeed, QUICKSORT takes quadratic time to sort the array

$(n, n-1, \ldots, 2, 1)$. Worse yet, it requires $O(n^2)$ time to process $(1, 2, \ldots, n - 1, n)$, which seems unnecessary since the array is already sorted.

The QUICKSORT algorithm so far seems like a bad imitation of MERGESORT. However, if we can choose a good "splitter" m that breaks an array into two equal parts, we might improve the running time. To achieve $O(n \log n)$ running time, it is not actually necessary to find a perfectly equal (50/50) split. For example, a split into approximately equal parts of size, say, 51/49 will also work. In fact, one can prove that the algorithm will achieve $O(n \log n)$ running time as long as the sets c_{small} and c_{large} are both larger in size than $n/4$.

It implies that, of n possible choices for m as elements of the array c, at least $\frac{3n}{4} - \frac{n}{4} = \frac{n}{2}$ of them make good splitters! In other words, if we randomly choose m (i.e., every element of the array c has the same probability to be chosen), there is at least a 50% chance that it will be a good splitter. This observation motivates the following randomized algorithm:

RANDOMIZEDQUICKSORT(c):
if c consists of a single element:
    return c
randomly select an element m from c
determine the set of elements c_{small} smaller than m
determine the set of elements c_{large} larger than m
RANDOMIZEDQUICKSORT(c_{small})
RANDOMIZEDQUICKSORT(c_{large})
combine c_{small}, m, and c_{large} into a single sorted array c_{sorted}
return c_{sorted}

RANDOMIZEDQUICKSORT is a fast algorithm in practice, but its worst case running time remains $O(n^2)$ since there is still a possibility that it selects bad splitters. Although the behavior of a randomized algorithm varies on the same input from one execution to the next, one can prove that its *expected* running time is $O(n \log n)$. The running time of a randomized algorithm is a *random variable*, and computer scientists are often interested in the mean value of this random variable which is referred to as the expected running time.

The key advantage of randomized algorithms is performance: for many practical problems randomized algorithms are faster (in the sense of expected running time) than the best known deterministic algorithms.

Another attractive feature of randomized algorithms, as illustrated by RANDOMIZEDQUICKSORT, is their simplicity.

We emphasize that RANDOMIZEDQUICKSORT, despite making random decisions, always returns the correct solution of the sorting problem. The only variable from one run to another is its running time, not the result. In contrast, other randomized algorithms usually produce incorrect (or, more gently, *approximate*) solutions. Randomized algorithms that always return correct answers are called *Las Vegas algorithms*, while algorithms that do not are called *Monte Carlo algorithms*. Of course, computer scientists prefer Las Vegas algorithms to Monte Carlo algorithms, but the former are often difficult to come by.

Chapter 3: Programming Challenges

To introduce you to our automated grading system, we will discuss two simple programming challenges and walk you through a step-by-step process of solving them. We will encounter several common pitfalls and will show you how to fix them.

Below is a brief overview of what it takes to solve a programming challenge in five steps:

Reading problem statement. Problem statement specifies the input-output format, the constraints for the input data as well as time and memory limits. Your goal is to implement a fast program that solves the problem and works within the time and memory limits.

Designing an algorithm. When the problem statement is clear, start designing an algorithm and don't forget to prove that it works correctly.

Implementing an algorithm. After you developed an algorithm, start implementing it in a programming language of your choice.

Testing and debugging your program. Testing is the art of revealing bugs. Debugging is the art of exterminating the bugs. When your program is ready, start testing it! If a bug is found, fix it and test again.

Submitting your program to the grading system. After testing and debugging your program, submit it to the grading system and wait for the message "Good job!". In the case you see a different message, return back to the previous stage.

3.1   Sum of Two Digits

Sum of Two Digits Problem
Compute the sum of two single digit numbers.

> **Input:** Two single digit numbers.
> **Output:** The sum of these numbers.

$$2 + 3 = 5$$

We start from this ridiculously simple problem to show you the pipeline of reading the problem statement, designing an algorithm, implementing it, testing and debugging your program, and submitting it to the grading system.

Input format. Integers a and b on the same line (separated by a space).

Output format. The sum of a and b.

Constraints. $0 \le a, b \le 9$.

Sample.

Input:

9 7

Output:

16

Time limits (sec.):

C++	Java	Python	C	C#	Haskell	JavaScript	Kotlin	Ruby	Rust	Scala
1	1.5	5	1	1.5	2	5	1.5	5	1	3

Memory limit. 512 Mb.

For this trivial problem, we will skip "Designing an algorithm" step and will move right to the pseudocode.

SumOfTwoDigits(a, b):
return $a + b$

Since the pseudocode does not specify how we input a and b, below we provide solutions in C++, Java, and Python3 programming languages as well as recommendations on compiling and running them. You can copy-and-paste the code to a file, compile/run it, test it on a few datasets, and then submit (the source file, not the compiled executable) to the grading system. Needless to say, we assume that you know the basics of one of programming languages that we use in our grading system.

C++

```cpp
#include <iostream>

int sum_of_two_digits(int first_digit, int second_digit) {
    return first_digit + second_digit;
}

int main() {
    int a = 0;
    int b = 0;
    std::cin >> a;
    std::cin >> b;
    std::cout << sum_of_two_digits(a, b);
    return 0;
}
```

Save this to a file (say, aplusb.cpp), compile it, run the resulting executable, and enter two numbers (on the same line).

Java

```java
import java.util.Scanner;

class SumOfTwoDigits {
    static int sumOfTwoDigits(int first_digit, int second_digit) {
        return first_digit + second_digit;
```

```
        }

    public static void main(String[] args) {
        Scanner s = new Scanner(System.in);
        int a = s.nextInt();
        int b = s.nextInt();
        System.out.println(sumOfTwoDigits(a, b));
    }
}
```

Save this to a file APlusB.java, compile it, run the resulting executable, and enter two numbers (on the same line).

Python3

```
# python3


def sum_of_two_digits(first_digit, second_digit):
    return first_digit + second_digit

if __name__ == '__main__':
    a, b = map(int, input().split())
    print(sum_of_two_digits(a, b))
```

Save this to a file (say, aplusb.py), run it, and enter two numbers on the same line. (The first line in the code above tells the grading system to use Python3 rather Python2.)

   Your goal is to implement an algorithm that produces a correct result under the given time and memory limits for any input satisfying the given constraints. You do not need to check that the input data satisfies the constraints, e.g., for the Sum of Two Digits Problem you do not need to check that the given integers *a* and *b* are indeed single digit integers (this is guaranteed).

3.2 Maximum Pairwise Product

Maximum Pairwise Product Problem
Find the maximum product of two distinct numbers in a sequence of non-negative integers.

> **Input:** A sequence of non-negative integers.
> **Output:** The maximum value that can be obtained by multiplying two different elements from the sequence.

	5	6	2	7	4
5		30	10	35	20
6	30		12	42	24
2	10	12		7	4
7	35	42	14		28
4	20	24	8	28	

Given a sequence of non-negative integers $a_1, \ldots, a_n$, compute

$$\max_{1 \le i \ne j \le n} a_i \cdot a_j.$$

Note that i and j should be different, though it may be the case that $a_i = a_j$.

Input format. The first line contains an integer n. The next line contains n non-negative integers $a_1, \ldots, a_n$ (separated by spaces).

Output format. The maximum pairwise product.

Constraints. $2 \le n \le 2 \cdot 10^5$; $0 \le a_1, \ldots, a_n \le 2 \cdot 10^5$.

Sample 1.
> Input:
> 3
> 1 2 3
> Output:
> 6

Sample 2.

Input:

10

7 5 14 2 8 8 10 1 2 3

Output:

140

Time and memory limits. The same as for the previous problem.

3.2.1   Naive Algorithm

A naive way to solve the Maximum Pairwise Product Problem is to go through all possible pairs of the input elements $A[1 \ldots n] = [a_1, \ldots, a_n]$ and to find a pair of distinct elements with the largest product:

MaxPairwiseProductNaive($A[1 \ldots n]$):
$product \leftarrow 0$
for i from 1 to n:
  for j from 1 to n:
    if $i \neq j$:
      if $product < A[i] \cdot A[j]$:
        $product \leftarrow A[i] \cdot A[j]$
return $product$

This code can be optimized and made more compact as follows.

MaxPairwiseProductNaive($A[1 \ldots n]$):
$product \leftarrow 0$
for i from 1 to n:
  for j from $i + 1$ to n:
    $product \leftarrow \max(product, A[i] \cdot A[j])$
return $product$

Implement this algorithm in your favorite programming language. If you are using C++, Java, or Python3, you may want to download the starter files (we provide starter solutions in these three languages for all the problems in the book). For other languages, you need to implement your solution from scratch.

Starter solutions for C++, Java, and Python3 are shown below.

C++

```cpp
#include <iostream>
#include <vector>
#include <algorithm>


int MaxPairwiseProduct(const std::vector<int>& numbers) {
    int max_product = 0;
    int n = numbers.size();

    for (int first = 0; first < n; ++first) {
        for (int second = first + 1; second < n; ++second) {
            max_product = std::max(max_product,
                numbers[first] * numbers[second]);
        }
    }

    return max_product;
}

int main() {
    int n;
    std::cin >> n;
    std::vector<int> numbers(n);
    for (int i = 0; i < n; ++i) {
        std::cin >> numbers[i];
    }

    int result = MaxPairwiseProduct(numbers);
    std::cout << result << "\n";
    return 0;
}
```

Java

```java
import java.util.*;
import java.io.*;

public class MaxPairwiseProduct {
    static int getMaxPairwiseProduct(int[] numbers) {
        int max_product = 0;
        int n = numbers.length;

        for (int first = 0; first < n; ++first) {
            for (int second = first + 1; second < n; ++second) {
                max_product = max(max_product,
                    numbers[first] * numbers[second])
            }
        }

        return max_product;
    }

    public static void main(String[] args) {
        FastScanner scanner = new FastScanner(System.in);
        int n = scanner.nextInt();
        int[] numbers = new int[n];
        for (int i = 0; i < n; i++) {
            numbers[i] = scanner.nextInt();
        }
        System.out.println(getMaxPairwiseProduct(numbers));
    }

    static class FastScanner {
        BufferedReader br;
        StringTokenizer st;

        FastScanner(InputStream stream) {
            try {
                br = new BufferedReader(new
                    InputStreamReader(stream));
            } catch (Exception e) {
                e.printStackTrace();
```

```
            }
        }

        String next() {
            while (st == null || !st.hasMoreTokens()) {
                try {
                    st = new StringTokenizer(br.readLine());
                } catch (IOException e) {
                    e.printStackTrace();
                }
            }
            return st.nextToken();
        }

        int nextInt() {
            return Integer.parseInt(next());
        }
    }

}
```

Python

```python
# python3


def max_pairwise_product(numbers):
    n = len(numbers)
    max_product = 0
    for first in range(n):
        for second in range(first + 1, n):
            max_product = max(max_product,
                              numbers[first] * numbers[second])

    return max_product


if __name__ == '__main__':
    input_n = int(input())
    input_numbers = [int(x) for x in input().split()]
```

```
print(max_pairwise_product(input_numbers))
```

After submitting this solution to the grading system, many students are surprised when they see the following message:

```
Failed case #4/17: time limit exceeded
```

After you submit your program, we test it on dozens of carefully designed test cases to make sure the program is fast and error proof. As the result, we usually know what kind of errors you made. The message above tells that the submitted program exceeds the time limit on the 4th out of 17 test cases.

Stop and Think. Why the solution does not fit into the time limit?

MAXPAIRWISEPRODUCTNAIVE performs of the order of n^2 steps on a sequence of length n. For the maximal possible value $n = 2 \cdot 10^5$, the number of steps is of the order $4 \cdot 10^{10}$. Since many modern computers perform roughly 10^8–10^9 basic operations per second (this depends on a machine, of course), it may take tens of seconds to execute MAXPAIRWISEPRODUCTNAIVE, exceeding the time limit for the Maximum Pairwise Product Problem.

We need a faster algorithm!

3.2.2 Fast Algorithm

In search of a faster algorithm, you play with small examples like [5, 6, 2, 7, 4]. Eureka—it suffices to multiply the two largest elements of the array—7 and 6!

Since we need to find the largest and the second largest elements, we need only two scans of the sequence. During the first scan, we find the largest element. During the second scan, we find the largest element among the remaining ones by skipping the element found at the previous scan.

MaxPairwiseProductFast($A[1 \ldots n]$):
  $index_1 \leftarrow 1$
  for i from 2 to n:
    if $A[i] > A[index_1]$:
      $index_1 \leftarrow i$
  $index_2 \leftarrow 1$
  for i from 2 to n:
    if $A[i] \neq A[index_1]$ and $A[i] > A[index_2]$:
      $index_2 \leftarrow i$
  return $A[index_1] \cdot A[index_2]$

3.2.3   Testing and Debugging

Implement this algorithm and test it using an input $A = [1, 2]$. It will output 2, as expected. Then, check the input $A = [2, 1]$. Surprisingly, it outputs 4. By inspecting the code, you find out that after the first loop, $index_1 = 1$. The algorithm then initializes $index_2$ to 1 and $index_2$ is never updated by the second for loop. As a result, $index_1 = index_2$ before the return statement. To ensure that this does not happen, you modify the pseudocode as follows:

MaxPairwiseProductFast($A[1 \ldots n]$):
  $index_1 \leftarrow 1$
  for i from 2 to n:
    if $A[i] > A[index_1]$:
      $index_1 \leftarrow i$
  if $index_1 = 1$:
    $index_2 \leftarrow 2$
  else:
    $index_2 \leftarrow 1$
  for i from 1 to n:
    if $A[i] \neq A[index_1]$ and $A[i] > A[index_2]$:
      $index_2 \leftarrow i$
  return $A[index_1] \cdot A[index_2]$

Check this code on a small datasets $[7, 4, 5, 6]$ to ensure that it produces correct results. Then try an input

```
2
100000 90000
```

You may find out that the program outputs something like $410\,065\,408$ or even a negative number instead of the correct result $9\,000\,000\,000$. If it does, this is most probably caused by an *integer overflow*. For example, in C++ programming language a large number like $9\,000\,000\,000$ does not fit into the standard int type that on most modern machines occupies 4 bytes and ranges from -2^{31} to $2^{31} - 1$, where

$$2^{31} = 2\,147\,483\,648.$$

Hence, instead of using the C++ int type you need to use the int64_t type when computing the product and storing the result. This will prevent integer overflow as the int64_t type occupies 8 bytes and ranges from -2^{63} to $2^{63} - 1$, where

$$2^{63} = 9\,223\,372\,036\,854\,775\,808.$$

You then proceed to testing your program on large data sets, e.g., an array $A[1\ldots2\cdot10^5]$, where $A[i] = i$ for all $1 \le i \le 2\cdot10^5$. There are two ways of doing this.

1. Create this array in your program and pass it to MAXPAIRWISEPRODUCTFAST (instead of reading it from the standard input).

2. Create a separate program, that writes such an array to a file dataset.txt. Then pass this dataset to your program from console as follows:

   ```
   yourprogram < dataset.txt
   ```

Check that your program processes this dataset within time limit and returns the correct result: $39\,999\,800\,000$. You are now confident that the program finally works!

However, after submitting it to the testing system, it fails again...

```
Failed case #5/17: wrong answer
```

But how would you generate a test case that make your program fail and help you to figure out what went wrong?

3.2.4 Can You Tell Me What Error Have I Made?

You are probably wondering why we did not provide you with the 5th out of 17 test datasets that brought down your program. The reason is that nobody will provide you with the test cases in real life!

Since even experienced programmers often make subtle mistakes solving algorithmic problems, it is important to learn how to catch bugs as early as possible. When the authors of this book started to program, they naively thought that nearly all their programs are correct. By now, we know that our programs are *almost never* correct when we first run them.

When you are confident that your program works, you often test it on just a few test cases, and if the answers look reasonable, you consider your work done. However, this is a recipe for a disaster. To make your program *always* work, you should test it on a set of carefully designed test cases. Learning how to implement algorithms as well as test and debug your programs will be invaluable in your future work as a programmer.

3.2.5 Stress Testing

We will now introduce *stress testing*—a technique for generating thousands of tests with the goal of finding a test case for which your solution fails.

A stress test consists of four parts:

1. Your implementation of an algorithm.

2. An alternative, trivial and slow, but correct implementation of an algorithm for the same problem.

3. A random test generator.

4. An infinite loop in which a new test is generated and fed into both implementations to compare the results. If their results differ, the test and both answers are output, and the program stops, otherwise the loop repeats.

The idea behind stress testing is that two correct implementations should give the same answer for each test (provided the answer to the problem is unique). If, however, one of the implementations is incorrect, then there exists a test on which their answers differ. The only case when it is not so is when there is the same mistake in both implementations, but that is unlikely (unless the mistake is somewhere in the input/output routines which are common to both solutions). Indeed, if one solution is correct and the other is wrong, then there exists a test case on which they differ. If both are wrong, but the bugs are different, then most likely there exists a test on which two solutions give different results.

Here is the the stress test for MaxPairwiseProductFast using MaxPairwiseProductNaive as a trivial implementation:

```
StressTest(N, M):
while true:
    n ← random integer between 2 and N
    allocate array A[1...n]
    for i from 1 to n:
        A[i] ← random integer between 0 and M
    print(A[1...n])
    result₁ ← MaxPairwiseProductNaive(A)
    result₂ ← MaxPairwiseProductFast(A)
    if result₁ = result₂:
        print("OK")
    else:
        print("Wrong answer: ", result₁, result₂)
        return
```

The while loop above starts with generating the length of the input sequence n, a random number between 2 and N. It is at least 2, because the problem statement specifies that $n \geq 2$. The parameter N should be small enough to allow us to explore many tests despite the fact that one of our solutions is slow.

After generating n, we generate an array A with n random numbers from 0 to M and output it so that in the process of the infinite loop we always know what is the current test; this will make it easier to catch an error in the test generation code. We then call two algorithms on A and compare the results. If the results are different, we print them and halt. Otherwise, we continue the while loop.

Let's run StressTest(10, 100 000) and keep our fingers crossed in a hope that it outputs "Wrong answer." We see something like this (the result can be different on your computer because of a different random number generator).

```
...
OK
67232 68874 69499
OK
6132 56210 45236 95361 68380 16906 80495 95298
OK
62180 1856 89047 14251 8362 34171 93584 87362 83341 8784
OK
21468 16859 82178 70496 82939 44491
OK
68165 87637 74297 2904 32873 86010 87637 66131 82858 82935
Wrong answer: 7680243769 7537658370
```

Hurrah! We've found a test case where MaxPairwiseProductNaive and MaxPairwiseProductFast produce different results, so now we can check what went wrong. Then we can debug this solution on this test case, find a bug, fix it, and repeat the stress test again.

Stop and Think. Do you see anything suspicious in the found dataset?

Note that generating tests automatically and running stress test is easy, but debugging is hard. Before diving into debugging, let's try to generate a smaller test case to simplify it. To do that, we change N from 10 to 5 and M from 100 000 to 9.

Stop and Think. Why did we first run StressTest with large parameters N and M and now intend to run it with small N and M?

We then run the stress test again and it produces the following.

```
...
7 3 6
OK
2 9 3 1 9
Wrong answer: 81 27
```

The slow MaxPairwiseProductNaive gives the correct answer 81 ($9 \cdot 9 = 81$), but the fast MaxPairwiseProductFast gives an incorrect answer 27.

Stop and Think. How MaxPairwiseProductFast can possibly return 27?

To debug our fast solution, let's check which two numbers it identifies as two largest ones. For this, we add the following line before the return statement of the MaxPairwiseProductFast function:

print($index_1$, $index_2$)

After running the stress test again, we see the following.

```
...
7 3 6
1 3
OK
5
2 9 3 1 9
2 3
Wrong answer: 81 27
```

Note that our solutions worked and then failed on exactly the same test cases as on the previous run of the stress test, because we didn't change anything in the test generator. The numbers it uses to generate tests are pseudorandom rather than random—it means that the sequence looks random, but it is the same each time we run this program. It is a convenient and important property, and you should try to have your programs exhibit such behavior, because deterministic programs (that always give the same result for the same input) are easier to debug than non-deterministic ones.

Now let's examine $index_1 = 2$ and $index_2 = 3$. If we look at the code for determining the second maximum, we will notice a subtle bug. When we implemented a condition on i (such that it is not the same as the previous maximum) instead of comparing i and $index_1$, we compared $A[i]$ with $A[index_1]$. This ensures that the second maximum differs from the first maximum by the value rather than by the index of the element that we select for solving the Maximum Pairwise Product Problem. So, our solution fails on any test case where the largest number is equal to the second largest number. We now change the condition from

$A[i] \neq A[index_1]$

to

$i \neq index_1$

After running the stress test again, we see a barrage of "OK" messages on the screen. We wait for a minute until we get bored and then decide that MaxPairwiseProductFast is finally correct!

However, you shouldn't stop here, since you have only generated very small tests with $N = 5$ and $M = 10$. We should check whether our program works for larger n and larger elements of the array. So, we change N to $1\,000$ (for larger N, the naive solution will be pretty slow, because its running time is quadratic). We also change M to $200\,000$ and run. We again see the screen filling with words "OK", wait for a minute, and then decide that (finally!) MAXPAIRWISEPRODUCTFAST is correct. Afterwards, we submit the resulting solution to the grading system and pass the Maximum Pairwise Product Problem test!

As you see, even for such a simple problems like Maximum Pairwise Product, it is easy to make subtle mistakes when designing and implementing an algorithm. The pseudocode below presents a more "reliable" way of implementing the algorithm.

MAXPAIRWISEPRODUCTFAST($A[1 \ldots n]$):
$index \leftarrow 1$
for i from 2 to n:
    if $A[i] > A[index]$:
        $index \leftarrow i$
swap $A[index]$ and $A[n]$
$index \leftarrow 1$
for i from 2 to $n - 1$:
    if $A[i] > A[index]$:
        $index \leftarrow i$
swap $A[index]$ and $A[n - 1]$
return $A[n - 1] \cdot A[n]$

In this book, besides learning how to design and analyze algorithms, you will learn how to implement algorithms in a way that minimizes the chances of making a mistake, and how to test your implementations.

3.2.6   Even Faster Algorithm

The MAXPAIRWISEPRODUCTFAST algorithm finds the largest and the second largest elements in about $2n$ comparisons.

Exercise Break. Find two largest elements in an array in $1.5n$ comparisons.

After solving this problem, try the next, even more challenging Exercise Break.

Exercise Break. Find two largest elements in an array in $n + \lceil \log_2 n \rceil - 2$ comparisons.

And if you feel that the previous Exercise Break was easy, here are the next two challenges that you may face at your next interview!

Exercise Break. Prove that no algorithm for finding two largest elements in an array can do this in less than $n + \lceil \log_2 n \rceil - 2$ comparisons.

Exercise Break. What is the fastest algorithm for finding three largest elements?

3.2.7 A More Compact Algorithm

The Maximum Pairwise Product Problem can be solved by the following compact algorithm that uses sorting (in non-decreasing order).

MaxPairwiseProductBySorting($A[1 \dots n]$):
Sort(A)
return $A[n-1] \cdot A[n]$

This algorithm does more than we actually need: instead of finding two largest elements, it sorts the entire array. For this reason, its running time is $O(n \log n)$, but not $O(n)$. Still, for the given constraints ($2 \le n \le 2 \cdot 10^5$) this is usually sufficiently fast to fit into a second and pass our grader.

3.3 Solving a Programming Challenge in Five Easy Steps

Below we summarize what we've learned in this chapter.

3.3.1 Reading Problem Statement

Start by reading the problem statement that contains the description of a computational task, time and memory limits, and a few sample tests.

Make sure you understand how an output matches an input in each sample case.

If time and memory limits are not specified explicitly in the problem statement, the following default values are used.

Time limits (sec.):

C++	Java	Python	C	C#	Haskell	JavaScript	Kotlin	Ruby	Rust	Scala
1	1.5	5	1	1.5	2	5	1.5	5	1	3

Memory limit: 512 Mb.

3.3.2 Designing an Algorithm

After designing an algorithm, prove that it is correct and try to estimate its expected running time on the most complex inputs specified in the constraints section. If you laptop performs roughly 10^8–10^9 operations per second, and the maximum size of a dataset in the problem description is $n = 10^5$, then an algorithm with quadratic running time is unlikely to fit into the time limit (since $n^2 = 10^{10}$), while a solution with running time $O(n \log n)$ will. However, an $O(n^2)$ solution will fit if $n = 1\,000$, and if $n = 100$, even an $O(n^3)$ solutions will fit. Although polynomial algorithms remain unknown for some hard problems in this book, a solution with $O(2^n n^2)$ running time will probably fit into the time limit as long as n is smaller than 20.

3.3.3 Implementing an Algorithm

Start implementing your algorithm in one of the following programming languages supported by our automated grading system: C, C++, C#, Haskell, Java, JavaScript, Kotlin, Python2, Python3, Ruby, Rust, or Scala. For all problems, we provide starter solutions for C++, Java, and Python3. For other programming languages, you need to implement a solution from scratch. The grading system detects the programming language of your submission automatically, based on the extension of the submission file.

We have reference solutions in C++, Java, and Python3 (that we don't share with you) which solve the problem correctly under the given constraints, and spend at most 1/3 of the time limit and at most 1/2 of the memory limit. You can also use other languages, and we've estimated the time limit multipliers for them. However, we have no guarantee that a correct solution for a particular problem running under the given time and memory constraints exists in any of those other languages.

In the Appendix, we list compiler versions and flags used by the grading system. We recommend using the same compiler flags when you test your solution locally. This will increase the chances that your program behaves in the same way on your machine and on the testing machine (note that a buggy program may behave differently when compiled by different compilers, or even by the same compiler with different flags).

3.3.4   Testing and Debugging

Submitting your implementation to the grading system without testing it first is a bad idea! Start with small datasets and make sure that your program produces correct results on all sample datasets. Then proceed to checking how long it takes to process a large dataset. To estimate the running time, it makes sense to implement your algorithm as a function like solve(dataset) and then implement an additional procedure generate() that produces a large dataset. For example, if an input to a problem is a sequence of integers of length $1 \leq n \leq 10^5$, then generate a sequence of length 10^5, pass it to your solve() function, and ensure that the program outputs the result quickly.

Check the boundary values to ensure that your program processes correctly both short sequences (e.g., with 2 elements) and long sequences (e.g., with 10^5 elements). If a sequence of integers from 0 to, let's say, 10^6 is given as an input, check how your program behaves when it is given a sequence $0, 0, \ldots, 0$ or a sequence $10^6, 10^6, \ldots, 10^6$. Afterwards, check it also on randomly generated data. Check degenerate cases like an empty set, three points on a single line, a tree which consists of a single path of nodes, etc.

After it appears that your program works on all these tests, proceed to stress testing. Implement a slow, but simple and correct algorithm and check that two programs produce the same result (note however that this is not applicable to problems where the output is not unique). Generate random test cases as well as biased tests cases such as those with only small numbers or a small range of large numbers, strings containing a single letter "a" or only two different letters (as opposed to strings composed of all possible Latin letters), and so on. Think about other possible tests which could be peculiar in some sense. For example, if you are generating graphs, try generating trees, disconnected graphs, complete graphs, bipartite graphs, etc. If you generate trees, try generating paths, binary trees, stars, etc. If you are generating integers, try generating both prime and composite numbers.

3.3.5 Submitting to the Grading System

When you are done with testing, submit your program to the grading system! Go to the submission page, create a new submission, and upload a file with your program (make sure to upload a source file rather than an executable). The grading system then compiles your program and runs it on a set of carefully constructed tests to check that it outputs a correct result for all tests and that it fits into the time and memory limits. The grading usually takes less than a minute, but in rare cases, when the servers are overloaded, it might take longer. Please be patient. You can safely leave the page when your solution is uploaded.

As a result, you get a feedback message from the grading system. You want to see the "Good job!" message indicating that your program passed all the tests. The messages "Wrong answer", "Time limit exceeded", "Memory limit exceeded" notify you that your program failed due to one of these reasons. If you program fails on one of the first two test cases, the grader will report this to you and will show you the test case and the output of your program. This is done to help you to get the input/output format right. In all other cases, the grader will *not* show you the test case where your program fails.

Chapter 4: Good Programming Practices

Programming is an art of not making off-by-one errors. In this chapter, we will describe some good practices for software implementation that will help you to avoid off-by-one bugs (OBOBs) and many other common programming pitfalls. Sticking to these good practices will help you to write a reliable, compact, readable, debuggable, and efficient code.

4.1 Language Independent

4.1.1 Code Format

LF1 Use code autoformatting of your favorite IDE (integrated development environment) or code editor. For example, many programmers use Eclipse, IDEA, PyCharm, Visual Studio.

LF2 Do not use spaces and tabs for indentation simultaneously. If the tab size changes, the code will be formatted ugly.

4.1.2 Code Structure

LS1 Structure your code. Structured programming paradigm is aimed at improving the clarity and reducing the development time of your programs by making extensive use of subroutines. Break your code into many subroutines such that each subroutine is responsible for a single task.

In particular, separate reading the input, computing the result, and writing the output. This makes it easier to update your code: e.g., later, the input format may change. This also makes it easier to test your code since computing the result in a separate function simplifies stress testing.

LS2 Avoid copy-pasting of one section of the code into another section. When copying a piece of code, you copy all its potential bugs. Instead of copying, add a new function (or class) and call it two times with different parameters.

47

LS3 Make your code compact if it does not reduce its readability. For example, if *condition* is a Boolean variable or expression then use the latter of the following two programs that achieve the same goal:

```
if condition:
    return true
else:
    return false
```

```
return condition
```

When computing the minimum number in an array, instead of

```
if current < minimum:
    minimum ← current
```

use

```
minimum ← min(minimum, current)
```

LS4 The scope of variables should be as small as possible.

LS5 When possible, prefer range-based `for` loops to index-based `for` loops. This will reduce the chance of an OBOB. For example, instead of

```
sumOfElements ← 0
for i from 0 to length(array) − 1:
    symOfElements ← sumOfElements + array[i]
```

use

```
sumOfElements ← 0
for each entry element in array:
    symOfElements ← sumOfElements + element
```

4.1.3 Names and Comments

LN1 Use meaningful names for variables. The length of a variable name should be proportional to the size of its scope, where the scope is defined as the part of the program where the variable is "visible." Using a name like *speed* instead of *s* will help your team members to read your program and will help you to debug it. Note that problem statements and mathematical formulas usually contain many single letter variables. This makes it tempting to use the same single letter names when implementing a program. At the same time, the styles of mathematical text and code differ a lot. In particular, formulas are surrounded by text, while code mainly consists of instructions.

A place where a short variable name is acceptable is a counter for a short loop. Still, if there are, say, two nested for loops, do not call the corresponding counters just *i* and *j* because it is difficult to catch a bug caused by using one of these counters instead of another. For the same reason, do not use variables like something1 and something2: it is easy to make a typo in the name of one of them and to get the other one. Instead, use names like something_first and something_second.

LN2 Likewise, use meaningful function names. Use verbs explaining what the function is supposed to do. Each function should be responsible for a single thing. If a natural name for your function contains two verbs (like ReadFromFileAndSort), this is a clear indicator to split it into two functions (ReadFromFile and Sort). If a function returns a Boolean value, name it like IsEmpty instead of just Empty.

LN3 Do not use comments to acquit bad variable names. Instead of calling a variable *n* and placing a comment like "number of balls", just call this variable *numberOfBalls*.

Comments to functions should be placed near their declaration rather than their implementation.

Avoid commented out code.

4.1.4   Debugging

LD1 Turn on compiler/interpreter warnings. Although inexperienced programmers sometimes view warnings as a nuisance, they help you to catch some bugs at the early stages of your software implementations.

LD2 Use assert statements. Each time, there is a condition that must be true at a certain point of your program, add a line

assert(condition)

A *postcondition* (*precondition*) is a statement that has to be true before (or after) the call to the function. It makes sense to state preconditions and postconditions for every function in your program. For example, it would save you time if you added a line

assert($index_1 \neq index_2$)

when implementing an algorithm for the Maximum Pairwise Product Problem in Section 3.2.2.

The assert statements can also be used to ensure that a certain point in your program is never reached. See the following pseudocode for computing the greatest common divisor of two positive integers.

GREATESTCOMMONDIVISOR(a, b):
assert($a \geq 1$ and $b \geq 1$)
for d from min(a, b) downto 1:
   if a mod $d = 0$ and b mod $d = 0$:
     return d
assert(False)

LD3 Do not optimize your code at early stages. As Donald Knuth once said, premature optimization is the root of all evil in programming.

Your code should be correct and should have the expected asymptotic running time. Do not apply any non-asymptotic optimizations before you ensure the correctness of your code. If your code is correct (in particular, it does not get the wrong answer feedback from the grader), but is still too slow (gets time limit exceeded message), start optimizing it. Measure its running time and locate bottlenecks in the code. Note that when compilers apply code optimization, even professional programmers have difficulties predicting bottlenecks.

4.1.5 Integers and Floating Point Numbers

LI1 Avoid integer overflow. Check the bounds on the input values, estimate the maximum value for the intermediate results and pick a sufficiently large numeric type.

When computing modulo m, take every intermediate result modulo m. Say, you want to compute the remainder of the product of all elements of *array* modulo 17. The naive way of doing this is the following.

> *product* ← 1
> for *element* in *array*:
>   *product* ← *product* · *element*
> return *product* mod 17

In languages with integer overflow (like C++ and Java) this will give a wrong result in many cases: even if *array* has only 100 elements and all its elements are equal to 2, the product does not fit into 64 bits. In languages with out-of-the-box long arithmetic, this code will be slower than needed (as product is getting larger at every iteration). The right way to compute the product is the following.

> *product* ← 1
> for *element* in *array*:
>   *product* ← (*product* · *element*) mod 17
> return *product*

LI2 Avoid floating point numbers whenever possible. In the Maximum Value of the Loot Problem (Section 6.2) you need to compare

$$\frac{p_i}{w_i} \text{ and } \frac{p_j}{w_j},$$

where p_i and p_j (w_i and w_j) are prices (weights) of two compounds. Instead of comparing these *rational* numbers, compare *integers* $p_i \cdot w_j$ and $p_j \cdot w_i$, since integers are faster to compute and precise. However, remember about integer overflow when computing products of large numbers!

In the Closest Points Problem (Section 7.6) you need to compare the distances between a pair of points (x_1, y_1) and (x_2, y_2) and a pair of points (x_3, y_3) and (x_4, y_4):

$$\sqrt{(x_1 - x_2)^2 + (y_1 - y_2)^2} \text{ and } \sqrt{(x_3 - x_4)^2 + (y_3 - y_4)^2}.$$

Instead of comparing these values, compare the values of their squares:

$$(x_1 - x_2)^2 + (y_1 - y_2)^2 \text{ and } (x_3 - x_4)^2 + (y_3 - y_4)^2.$$

In fact, in this problem you need to deal with non-integer numbers just once: only when you output the result.

4.1.6 Ranges

LR1 Use 0-based arrays. Even if the problem statement specifies a 1-based sequence $a_1, \ldots, a_n$, store it in a 0-based array $A[0..n-1]$ (such that $A[i] = a_{i-1}$) instead of a 1-based array $A[0..n]$ (such that $A[i] = a_i$). In most programming languages, arrays are 0-based. A 0-based array contains only the input data, while an array $A[0..n]$ contains a dummy element $A[0]$ that you may accidentally use in your program. For this reason, the size of a 0-based array is equal to the number of input elements making it easier to iterate through it.

To illustrate this point, compare the following two implementations of a function that reads an integer n followed by reading integers $a_1, a_2, \ldots, a_n$. Although this section discusses language-independent good programming practices, we take a liberty to present two Python implementations

The first implementation uses a 1-based array A.

```
n = int(stdin.readline())
A = [None] * (n + 1)
```

```
for i in range(1, n + 1):
    A[i] = int(stdin.readline())
```

The second one uses a 0-based array A.

```
n = int(stdin.readline())
A = [None] * n
for i in range(len(A)):
    A[i] = int(stdin.readline())
```

The former version has more places for potential OBOBs.

LR2 Use semiopen intervals to avoid OBOBs. A *semiopen* interval includes the left boundary and excludes the right boundary: $[l,r) = \{l, l+1, \ldots, r-1\}$.

Recall that the MERGESORT algorithm first sorts the left half of the given array, then sorts the second half, and finally merges the results. The recursive implementation of this algorithm, given below, takes an array A as well as two indices l and r and sorts the subarray $A[l..r]$. That is, it sorts the *closed* interval $[l,r] = \{l, l+1, \ldots, r\}$ of A that includes both boundaries l and r.

MERGESORT(A, l, r):
if $r - l + 1 \le 1$:
   return
$m \leftarrow \lfloor \frac{l+r}{2} \rfloor$
MERGESORT(A, l, m)
MERGESORT($A, m+1, r$)
MERGE(A, l, m, r)

Using *semiopen* instead of closed intervals reduces the chances of making an OBOB, because:

(a) The number of elements in a semiopen interval $[l,r)$ is $r-l$ (for a closed interval $[l,r]$, it is $r-l+1$).

(b) It is easy to split a semiopen interval into two semiopen intervals: $[l,r) = [l,m) \cup [m,r)$ (for a closed interval $[l,r]$, $[l,r] = [l,m] \cup [m+1,r]$).

Compare the previous implementation with the following one.

$\textsc{MergeSort}(A, l, r)$:
if $r - l \leq 1$:
    return
$m \leftarrow l + \lfloor \frac{r-l}{2} \rfloor$
$\textsc{MergeSort}(A, l, m)$
$\textsc{MergeSort}(A, m, r)$
$\textsc{Merge}(A, l, m, r)$

For an array $A[0..n-1]$, the outer call for the first implementation is $\textsc{MergeSort}(A, 0, n-1)$, while for the second one it is $\textsc{MergeSort}(A, 0, n)$.

4.2   C++ Specific

4.2.1   Code Format

CF1   Stick to a specific code style. Mixing various code styles in your programs make them less readable. Select your favorite code style and always follow it. Recommended style guides:

- C++ Core Guidelines by Bjarne Stroustrup and Herb Sutter: `https://github.com/isocpp/CppCoreGuidelines/blob/master/CppCoreGuidelines.md`

- Google C++ Style Guide: `http://google.github.io/styleguide/cppguide.html`

CF2   Be consistent. For example, either *always* put the opening curly bracket on the same line as the definition of a class or a function or *never* do it.

CF3   There are many ways of formatting C++ code and there is no universal way at the same time. It is important to be consistent (recall CF2). A simple and reasonable way of achieving this is autoformatting your code using `clang-format`.

4.2.2   Code Structure

CS1 Avoid statements of the form using namespace foo. This may potentially lead to name clashes (if, say, you implement your own min method) that will, in turn, lead to bugs that are difficult to catch. Moreover, this violates the general principle of using namespaces.

   If you use std::vector and std::cin heavily in your program, instead of

```
using namespace std;
```

   write

```
using std::vector;
using std::cin;
```

CS2 Avoid using old-style scanf and printf. Instead, use std::cin and std::cout.

   For compatibility reasons, iostream synchronizes with stdio (which makes it possible to use both interfaces for input/output). Turning it off makes std::cin and std::cout work several times faster:

```
#include <iostream>

int main() {
    std::ios_base::sync_with_stdio(false);
    ...
    return 0;
}
```

   This might be noticeable when, say, you output 10^5 integers.

CS3 Other things being equal, use pre-increment ++i instead of post-increment i++. For integer types there is no difference, but for more complex iterators, the post-increment creates a copy of an object which, in turn, consumes more memory and slows down a program. At the same time, prefer range-based for loops when possible (see LS5).

CS4 Use const each time when it makes sense. This allows to catch some bugs at the compilation stage and serves as an additional documentation of your code.

CS5 Pass input parameters to a function by value in case they are of primitive types like bool, double, or int32_t. For more complex types of input parameters, pass them by a constant reference to avoid unnecessary copying.

CS6 When possible, use C++ constructions instead of the corresponding C constructions: e.g., std::copy/std::copy_n and std::fill/std::fill_n instead of std::memcpy and std::memset; <limits> instead of <climits>.

CS7 When using an external function or type, don't forget to include the corresponding header.

CS8 Each variable should be used for a single purpose. Do not use auxiliary variable likes tmp in various parts of your code. In most cases, variables containing tmp or temp in their names are either useless or named badly.

CS9 Declare variables as close as possible to their first usage. This makes your code easier to read. Always initialize variables when declaring them (or immediately after declaration). Avoid using global variables and make each variable as local as possible (recall LS4): if it is used only in a function, it should be local for the function; if it is used only in a cycle, it should be local for the cycle. This allows to reduce the number of variables that should be kept in mind when reading your code.

CS10 Use the limits header to check ranges.

CS11 Do not use std::pair. This makes it difficult to read the code: each time a pair is used the reader has to go back to the definition of the pair to check what do first and second mean. Moreover, it is particularly easy to confuse first and second in your code. Instead of a pair, define your own struct with appropriately named fields.

The only exception of this rule is a case when a pair is used in a local piece of code that fits to one screen. In this case it could be convenient to use a pair since it has a default comparing operator (that can be used, e.g., for sorting). The fact that it is only used in a short piece of code does not confuse the reader.

CS12 Do not use define for declaring functions. Instead, use template or inline functions.

CS13 C headers (with .h extension like <stdio.h>, <math.h>) are present in C++ due to backward compatibility only. Instead of them, use the corresponding C++ headers (like <cstdio>, <cmath>).

4.2.3 Types and Constants

CT1 For Boolean type, use the bool type instead of int.

CT2 Avoid using the following standard types: short, long long, signed char, unsigned short, unsigned, and unsigned long long. Prefer int32_t and int64_t types (from the cstdint header) that are *guaranteed* to be 32 and 64 bit integers, respectively. Avoid using less than 32 bit types.

CT3 Do not subtract from an operand of unsigned type if you haven't verified that this will not lead to an overflow.

To illustrate this, assume that you need to iterate through all but the last five elements of container. The following code results in an undefined behavior in case container has less then five elements:

```
for (int i = 0; i < container.size() - 5; ++i) {
    ...
}
```

A safer way of doing this is the following:

```
for (std::size_t i = 0; i + 5 < container.size(); ++i) {
    ...
}
```

CT4 Avoid using `int[]` and `int*` for arrays. Use `std::vector` instead. Similarly, instead of C-type strings `char[]` and `char*`, use `std::string`.

CT5 Use C++ type cast (`static_cast<int>(x)`) instead of C (`((int)x)` or functional style (`int(x)`) type cast (especially, in template code).

CT6 Do not use macros for defining constants. Instead of

```
#define MAX_LENGTH 100000
```

use either

```
constexpr int32_t kMaxLength = 100000;
```

or

```
const int32_t kMaxLength = 100000;
```

CT7 Use the following zero constants for various types: 0 for integer types, 0.0 for floating point types, `nullptr` for pointers, `'\0'` as null char.

CT8 Do not use magic constants in your code. Consider, e.g., the case when you need to iterate through all letters of an alphabet. Instead of

```
for (char letter = 'a'; letter <= 'z'; ++letter) {
    ...
}
```

use

```
const char FIRST_LETTER = 'a';
const char LAST_LETTER = 'z';
...
for (char letter = FIRST_LETTER; letter <= LAST_LETTER; ++letter) {
    ...
}
```

4.2.4 Classes

CC1 Differentiate class and struct (though the only formal difference between them is whether fields are public by default or not). Use struct when you need a bunch of *public* fields with no non-trivial methods. Use a class as a bunch of *private* fields with methods processing them. Example of a struct:

```
struct Point {
    double x;
    double y;
};

bool operator < (const Point& first, const Point& second) {
    if (first.x != second.x) {
        return first.x < second.x;
    }
    return first.y < second.y;
}
```

Example of a class:

```
class Path {
public:
    Path(double time, double average_speed)
        : time_(time), average_speed_(average_speed)
    {}

    double Time() const {
        return time_;
    }

    double AverageSpeed() const {
        return average_speed_;
    }

    double Distance() const {
        return time_ * average_speed_;
    }

private:
    double time_;
```

```
        double average_speed_;
};
```

CC2 When you need to compare objects of your class or struct, implement
     just operator<, but don't implement other operators for comparing
     (operator<=, operator>, operator>=). The reason is that the other
     comparing operators are implied by operator<. Following this con-
     vention will decrease code duplication and make your program more
     readable.

     If using standard C++2a, implement operator<=>.

CC3 When using member initializer lists in constructors, list the mem-
     bers in exactly the same order they are declared in the class defini-
     tion. The reason is that the members are always initialized in order
     they are declared (rather than in the order they are listed). Hence,
     using different order may lead to difficult to catch bugs. E.g., the
     following code leads to undefined behavior.

```
struct DataHolder {
    explicit DataHolder(size_t size):
        data(size),
        current(&data[0])
    {}

    int* current;
    std::vector<int> data;
};
```

CC4 Use explicit specifier for constructors with one argument (to avoid
     implicit conversion and copy-initialization).

CC5 Use final and override specifiers whenever possible.

CC6 Use a separate naming style for private class members to make it
     easy to distinguish them from method parameters. One of the com-
     mon conventions is to use either an underscore as a suffix (like name_)
     or the prefix m_ (like m_name). Do not start the names with an under-
     score.

4.2.5 Containers

CCO1 Avoid using dynamically allocated variables explicitly (via new and malloc). This leads to memory leaks in case you forget to call delete or free. Moreover, new is quite slow, hence allocate small variables on stack. For allocating data of size that is unknown in advance, use standard containers (like std::vector).

CCO2 When using standard containers, remember that they have various constructors, assignment operators, and other convenient methods. E.g., the following code creates an $n \times m$ 2d-array (i.e., a matrix) filled in by 100's.

```
std::vector< vector<int32_t> > cache(
  n,
  std::vector<int32_t>(m, 100));
```

The following code swaps two vectors without copying the whole contents:

```
std::vector<int32_t> first(1000000, 1);
std::vector<int32_t> second(2000000, 2);
first.swap(second);
```

4.2.6 Integers and Floating Point Numbers

CI1 Use double type for floating type numbers.

CI2 To compute the absolute value of a double, use std::abs from cmath header.

CI3 Do not compare float or double numbers using <, >, <=, >=, or ==. The reason is that there is a precision loss when working with real numbers. Because of this, two sequences of operations that should lead to the same real number may result in different float/double numbers. A safer way of comparing float/double numbers is the following.

```
const double COMPARISON_THRESHOLD = 1e-8;

bool isLess(double first, double second) {
```

```
    return first < second - COMPARISON_THRESHOLD;
}

bool isLessOrEqual(double first, double second) {
  return first < second + COMPARISON_THRESHOLD;
}

bool isEqual(double first, double second) {
  return std::abs(first - second) < COMPARISON_THRESHOLD;
}
```

CI4 For generating random numbers, use functions from the random
    header instead of the function std::rand(). Note that std::rand()
    generates integers not exceeding RAND_MAX. The value of RAND_MAX
    differs between different compilers.

4.3   Python Specific

4.3.1   General

PG1 Follow PEP-8 style guide: https://www.python.org/dev/peps/
    pep-0008/. Use pep8 (https://pypi.python.org/pypi/pep8) and
    autopep8 (https://pypi.python.org/pypi/autopep8) tools.

PG2 List imported modules in the beginning of a file. List them in the
    lexicographic order.

```
# bad
import gzip
import sys
from collections import defaultdict
import io
from contextlib import contextmanager
import functools
from urllib.request import urlopen

# good
import functools
import gzip
```

```
import io
import sys
from collections import defaultdict
from contextlib import contextmanager
from urllib.request import urlopen
```

PG3 Use operators is and is_not for comparing with singletones (like
None) only. The only exception is Boolean constants True and False.

PG4 Use *falsy/truthy* semantics. *Falsy* values: None; False; zeroes 0, 0.0,
and 0j; empty strings and bytes; empty collections.

```
# bad
if acc == []:
    ...

# bad
if len(acc) > 0:
    ...

# good
if not acc:
    ...

# ok
if acc == 0:
    ...
```

PG5 Avoid unnecessary copying.

```
# bad
xs = set([x**2 for x in range(42)])

for x in list(sorted(xs)):
    ...

# good
xs = {x**2 for x in range(42)}

for x in sorted(xs):
    ...
```

PG6 Do not use the method dict.get(), do not use a collection dict.keys to check whether a key is present in dict, do not use dict.keys to iterate over a dictionary.

```
# bad
if key in dict.keys():
    ...

if not dict.get(key, False):
    ...

# good
if key in dict:
    ...

if key not in dict:
    ...

# bad
for key in dict.keys():
    ...

# good
for key in dict:
    ...
```

PG7 Use literals for creating empty collections. The only exception is set: there is no literal for an empty set in Python.

```
# bad
dict(), list(), tuple()

# good
{}, [], ()
```

PG8 In Python3, use // for integer division.

PG9 Use float("inf") for infinity.

PG10 If needed, increase the recursion depth as follows. (Note that to take advantage of bigger stack, one need to launch the computation in a new thread.)

```
sys.setrecursionlimit(10**7)
threading.stack_size(2**27)
threading.Thread(target=main).start()
```

4.3.2   Code Structure

PC1 Do not emulate `for` loop.

```
# bad
i = 0
while i < n:
    ...
    i += 1

# good
for i in range(n):
    ...
```

PC2 Prefer range-based loops (see LS5). If an index is necessary, use enumerate.

```
# bad
for i in range(len(xs)) :
    x = xs[i]

# good
for x in xs:
    ...

# good
for i, x in enumerate(xs):
    ...

# bad
for i in range(min(len(xs), len(ys))):
    f(xs[i], ys[i])

# good
for x, y in zip(xs, ys):
    f(x, y)
```

PC3 Do not use meaningless if and ternary operators (see LS3).

```
# bad
xs = [x for x in xs if predicate]
return True if xs else False

# good
xs = [x for x in xs if predicate]
return bool(xs)

# good
return any(map(predicate, xs))
```

PC4 Do not use file.readline and file.readlines for iterating over
a file.

```
# bad
while True:
    line = file.readline()
    ...

for line in file.readlines():
    ...

# good
for line in file:
    ...
```

4.3.3 Functions

PF1 Avoid mutable default values.

PF2 Do not overuse functional idioms. In many cases, generators are
more readable than a mix of map, filter, and zip.

```
# bad
list(map(lambda x: x ** 2,
         filter(lambda x: x % 2 == 1,
                range(10))))

# good
[x ** 2 for x in range(10) if x % 2 == 1]
```

PF3 Do not overuse generators. In many cases, a `for` loop is more readable.

PF4 Avoid meaningless anonymous functions.

```
# bad
map(lambda x: frobnicate(x), xs)

# good
map(frobnicate, xs)

# bad
collections.defaultdict(lambda: [])

# good
collections.defaultdict(list)
```

4.3.4 Strings

PS1 Use `str.startswith` and `str.endswith`.

```
# bad
s[:len(p)] == p
s.find(p) == len(s) - len(p)

# good
s.startswith(p)
s.endswith(p)
```

PS2 Use string formatting instead of concatenation of results of `str`.

```
# bad
"(+ " + str(expr1) + " " + str(expr2) + ")"

# good
"(+ {} {})".format(expr1, expr2)
```

Exception: converting a single parameter to a string.

```
# bad
"{}".format(value)
```

```
# good
str(value)
```

PS3 Simplify formatting expressions when possible.

```
# bad
"(+ {0} {1})"
"(+ {expr1} {expr2})"

# good
"(+ {} {})"
```

PS4 Keep in mind that str.format converts its parameters to strings.

```
# bad
"(+ {} {})".format(str(expr1), str(expr2))

# good
"(+ {} {})".format(expr1, expr2)
```

4.3.5 Classes

PCL1 Use collections.namedtuple as a collection of immutable fields.

```
# bad
class Point:
    def __init__(self, x, y):
        self.x = x
        self.y = y

# good
Point = namedtuple("Point", ["x", "y"])
```

PCL2 Avoid calling "magic methods" when there is an appropriate function or operator.

```
# bad
expr.__str__()
expr.__add__(other)

# good
```

```
str(expr)
expr + other
```

PCL3 Instead of using `type` for checking whether a given object has a required type, use the function `isinstance`.

```
# bad
type(instance) == Point
type(instance) is Point

# good
isinstance(instance, Point)
```

4.3.6   Exceptions

PE1 Keep the size of `try` and `with` blocks as small as possible.

PE2 Use `except Exception` rather than `except BaseException` or except for catching an exception.

PE3 Use the most specific type of exception in the `except` block.

```
# bad
try:
    mapping[key]
except Exception:
    ...

# good
try:
    mapping[key]
except KeyError:
    ...
```

PE4 Inherit your own exceptions from `Exception` rather than `BaseException`.

PE5 Use context managers instead of `try-finally`.

```
# bad
handle = open("path/to/file")
```

```
try:
    do_something(handle)
finally:
    handle.close()

# good
with open("path/to/file") as handle:
    do_something(handle)
```

Chapter 5: Algorithmic Warm Up

In this chapter, you will learn that programs based on efficient algorithms can be a billion time faster than programs based on naive algorithms. You will learn how to estimate the running time and memory of an algorithm without ever implementing it. Armed with this knowledge, you will be able to compare various algorithms, select the most efficient ones, and finally implement them to solve various programming challenges! In each chapter, we give a solution of one of the problems that is shown below in a bold rectangle.

Fibonacci Number	Last Digit of Fibonacci Number	Greatest Common Divisor
$F_n = F_{n-1} + F_{n-2}$	$F_{170} = 150\,804\,340\,016$ $807\,970\,735\,635$ $273\,952\,047\,185$	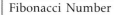

Least Common Multiple	Fibonacci Number Again	Last Digit of the Sum of Fibonacci Numbers
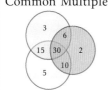	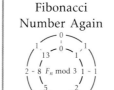	$1 + 1 + 2 + 3 + 5 + 8 = 20$

Last Digit of the Sum of Fibonacci Numbers Again	Last Digit of the Sum of Squares of Fibonacci Numbers
$2 + 3 + 5 + 8 + 13 = 31$	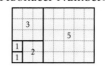

5.1   Fibonacci Number

Fibonacci Number Problem
Compute the n-th Fibonacci number.

     Input: An integer n.$\qquad\qquad$ $F_n = F_{n-1} + F_{n-2}$
     Output: n-th Fibonacci number.

Fibonacci numbers are defined recursively:

$$F_n = \begin{cases} n & \text{if } n \text{ is 0 or 1} \\ F_{n-1} + F_{n-2} & \text{if } n \geq 2 \end{cases}$$

resulting in the following recursive algorithm:

FIBONACCI(n):
if $n \leq 1$:
   return n
return FIBONACCI($n-1$) + FIBONACCI($n-2$)

Implement this algorithm and try to compute F_{40}. You will see that it already takes significant time. And the Sun may die before your computer returns F_{150} since modern computers need billions of years to compute this number...

To understand why this algorithm is so slow, try computing F_{20} at http://www.cs.usfca.edu/~galles/visualization/DPFib.html.

Enter "20" and press the "Fibonacci Recursive" button. You will see a seemingly endless series of recursive calls. Now, press "Skip Forward" to stop the recursive algorithm and call the iterative algorithm by pressing "Fibonacci Table". This will instantly compute F_{20}. (Note that the visualization uses a slightly different definition of Fibonacci numbers: $F_0 = 1$ instead of $F_0 = 0$.)

Input format. An integer n.

Output format. F_n.

Constraints. $0 \le n \le 45$.

Sample 1.

    Input:
    3
    Output:
    2

Sample 2.

    Input:
    10
    Output:
    55

Time and memory limits. When time/memory limits are not specified, we use the default values specified in Section 3.3.1.

5.2   Last Digit of Fibonacci Number

Last Digit of Fibonacci Number Problem
Compute the last digit of the n-th Fibonacci number.

Input: An integer $0 \leq n \leq 10^6$.
Output: The last digit of the n-th Fibonacci number.

$F_{170} = 150\,804\,340\,016$
$807\,970\,735\,635$
$273\,952\,047\,185$

To solve this problem, let's compute F_n and simply output its last digit:

FIBONACCILASTDIGIT(n):
$F[0] \leftarrow 0$
$F[1] \leftarrow 1$
for i from 2 to n:
  $F[i] \leftarrow F[i-1] + F[i-2]$
return $F[n]$ mod 10

Note that Fibonacci numbers grow fast. For example,

$$F_{100} = 354\,224\,848\,179\,261\,915\,075.$$

Therefore, if you use C++ int32_t or int64_t types for storing F, you will quickly hit an integer overflow. If you reach out for arbitrary precision numbers, like Java's BigInteger, or Pythons built-in integers, you'll notice that the loop runs much slower when the iteration number increases.

To get around this issue, instead of storing the i-th Fibonacci number in $F[i]$ we will store just the last digit of F_i, i.e., we replace the body of the for loop with the following:

$F[i] \leftarrow (F[i-1] + F[i-2])$ mod 10

Afterwards, computing the sum of single digit numbers $F[i-1]$ and $F[i-2]$ will be fast.

Input format.   An integer n.

Output format. The last digit of F_n.

Constraints. $0 \le n \le 10^6$.

Sample 1.

    Input:

    3

    Output:

    2

    $F_3 = 2$.

Sample 2.

    Input:

    139

    Output:

    1

    $F_{139} = 50\,095\,301\,248\,058\,391\,139\,327\,916\,261$.

Sample 3.

    Input:

    91239

    Output:

    6

    $F_{91\,239}$ will take more than ten pages to represent, but its last digit is equal to 6.

5.3   Greatest Common Divisor

Greatest Common Divisor Problem
Compute the greatest common divisor of two positive integers.

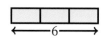

   Input: Two positive integers.
   Output: Their greatest common divisor.

The greatest common divisor $GCD(a, b)$ of two positive integers a and b is the largest integer d that divides both a and b. The solution of the Greatest Common Divisor Problem was first described (but not discovered!) by the Greek mathematician Euclid twenty three centuries ago. But the name of a mathematician who discovered this algorithm, a century before Euclid described it, remains unknown. Centuries later, Euclid's algorithm was rediscovered by Indian and Chinese astronomers. Now, efficient algorithm for computing the greatest common divisor is an important ingredient of modern cryptographic algorithms.

Your goal is to implement Euclid's algorithm for computing GCD.

Input format. Integers a and b (separated by a space).

Output format. $GCD(a, b)$.

Constraints. $1 \le a, b \le 2 \cdot 10^9$.

Sample.

   Input:
   28851538 1183019
   Output:
   17657
   $28851538 = 17657 \cdot 1634, 1183019 = 17657 \cdot 67.$

5.4   Least Common Multiple

Least Common Multiple Problem
Compute the least common multiple of two positive integers.

> **Input:** Two positive integers.
> **Output:** Their least common multiple.

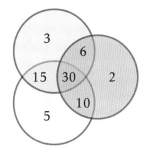

The least common multiple LCM(a, b) of two positive integers a and b is the smallest integer m that is divisible by both a and b.

Stop and Think. How LCM(a, b) is related to GCD(a, b)?

Input format. Integers a and b (separated by a space).

Output format. LCM(a, b).

Constraints. $1 \le a, b \le 2 \cdot 10^9$.

Sample 1.

Input:
6 8

Output:
24

Among all positive integers that are divisible by both 6 and 8 (e.g., 48, 480, 24), 24 is the smallest one.

Sample 2.

Input:
28851538 1183019

Output:
1933053046

1 933 053 046 is the smallest positive integer divisible by both 28 851 538 and 1 183 019.

5.5   Fibonacci Number Again

Fibonacci Number Again Problem
Compute the n-th Fibonacci number modulo m.

> **Input:** Integers $0 \le n \le 10^{18}$ and $2 \le m \le 10^5$.
> **Output:** n-th Fibonacci modulo m.

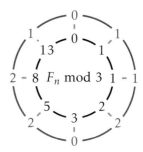

In this problem, n may be so huge that an algorithm looping for n iterations will be too slow. Therefore we need to avoid such a loop. To get an idea how to solve this problem without going through all Fibonacci numbers F_i for i from 0 to n, take a look at the table below:

i	0	1	2	3	4	5	6	7	8	9	10	11	12	13	14	15
F_i	0	1	1	2	3	5	8	13	21	34	55	89	144	233	377	610
$F_i \bmod 2$	0	1	1	0	1	1	0	1	1	0	1	1	0	1	1	0
$F_i \bmod 3$	0	1	1	2	0	2	2	1	0	1	1	2	0	2	2	1

Stop and Think. Do you see any interesting properties of the last two rows in the table above?

Both these sequences are periodic! For $m = 2$, the period is 011 and has length 3, while for $m = 3$ the period is 01120221 and has length 8.

i	0	1	2	3	4	5	6	7	8	9	10	11	12	13	14	15
F_i	0	1	1	2	3	5	8	13	21	34	55	89	144	233	377	610
$F_i \bmod 2$	0	1	1	0	1	1	0	1	1	0	1	1	0	1	1	0
$F_i \bmod 3$	0	1	1	2	0	2	2	1	0	1	1	2	0	2	2	1

Therefore, to compute, say, $F_{2015} \bmod 3$ we just need to find the remainder of 2015 when divided by 8. Since $2015 = 251 \cdot 8 + 7$, we conclude that $F_{2015} \bmod 3 = F_7 \bmod 3 = 1$.

It turns out that for any integer $m \geq 2$, the sequence F_n mod m is periodic. The period always starts with 01 and is known as *Pisano period* (Pisano is another name of Fibonacci).

Exercise Break. What is the period of F_i mod 5?

Exercise Break. Prove that F_i mod m is periodic for every m.

Exercise Break. Prove that the period of F_i mod m does not exceed m^2.

Input format. Integers n and m.

Output format. F_n mod m.

Constraints. $1 \leq n \leq 10^{18}$, $2 \leq m \leq 10^5$.

Sample 1.

   Input:

   1 239

   Output:

   1

   F_1 mod 239 = 1 mod 239 = 1.

Sample 2.

   Input:

   115 1000

   Output:

   885

   F_{115} mod 1000 = 483 162 952 612 010 163 284 885 mod 1000 = 885.

Sample 3.

   Input:

   2 816 213 588 239

   Output:

   151

   $F_{2 816 213 588}$ would require hundreds pages to write it down, but $F_{2 816 213 588}$ mod 239 = 151.

5.6   Last Digit of the Sum of Fibonacci Numbers

Last Digit of the Sum of Fibonacci Numbers Problem

Compute the last digit of $F_0 + F_1 + \cdots + F_n$.

Input: Integer $0 \leq n \leq 10^{18}$.

Output: The last digit of $F_0 + F_1 + \cdots + F_n$.

$1 + 1 + 2 + 3 + 5 + 8 = 20$

Hint.   Since the brute force approach for this problem is too slow, try to come up with a formula for $F_0 + F_1 + F_2 + \cdots + F_n$. Play with small values of n to get an insight and use a solution for the previous problem afterwards.

Input format.   Integer n.

Output format. $(F_0 + F_1 + \cdots + F_n) \bmod 10$.

Constraints. $0 \leq n \leq 10^{18}$.

Sample 1.

Input:

3

Output:

4

$F_0 + F_1 + F_2 + F_3 = 0 + 1 + 1 + 2 = 4$.

Sample 2.

Input:

100

Output:

5

$F_0 + \cdots + F_{100} = 927\,372\,692\,193\,078\,999\,175$.

Solution

The table below shows the first eleven Fibonacci numbers and the first eleven numbers $S_n = F_0 + F_1 + \cdots + F_n$.

n	0	1	2	3	4	5	6	7	8	9	10
F_n	0	1	1	2	3	5	8	13	21	34	55
S_n	0	1	2	4	7	12	20	33	54	88	143

Stop and Think. Do you see any similarities between sequences $F_0, \ldots, F_{10}$ and $S_0, \ldots, S_{10}$?

It looks like $S_n = F_{n+2} - 1$ — let's prove it by induction. This condition certainly holds for the base step ($n = 0$) since $S_0 = F_2 - 1$. For the induction step, let's assume that the statement holds for $0, 1, \ldots, n$ and prove it for $n + 1$:

$$S_{n+1} = F_0 + F_1 + \cdots + F_n + F_{n+1} = S_n + F_{n+1} = F_{n+2} - 1 + F_{n+1} = F_{n+3} - 1.$$

Another way of arriving to the formula $S_n = F_{n+2} - 1$ is to sum up the equalities

$$
\begin{aligned}
F_n &= F_{n+2} &-& F_{n+1} \\
F_{n-1} &= F_{n+1} &-& F_n \\
F_{n-2} &= F_n &-& F_{n-1} \\
&\ \ \vdots \\
F_2 &= F_4 &-& F_3 \\
F_1 &= F_3 &-& F_2 \\
F_0 &= F_2 &-& F_1
\end{aligned}
$$

Since the identically colored terms cancel out, the sum of all terms on the left is S_n and the sum of all terms on the right is $F_{n+2} - F_1 = F_{n+2} - 1$.

Thus, the problem reduces to finding the last digit of $F_{n+2} - 1$. However, since n can be as large as 10^{18}, we need to compute the last digit of $F_{n+2} - 1$ without explicitly going through $F_0, F_1, \ldots, F_{n+2}$.

Stop and Think. How can we find out the last digit of the n-th Fibonacci number without checking the last digits of all n smaller Fibonacci numbers?

Computing the Last Digit of a Fibonacci Number Using Pisano Period

The table below illustrates that the sequence F_n mod 10 is periodic — the last digits repeat themselves with a period 60 known as the *Pisano period* (see the Fibonacci Number Again Problem). In other words:

$$F_n \bmod 10 = F_{n \bmod 60} \bmod 10.$$

For example,

$$F_{2000} \bmod 10 = F_{2000 \bmod 60} \bmod 10 = F_{20} \bmod 10 = 6765 \bmod 10 = 5.$$

n	0	1	2	3	4	5	6	7	$\cdots$	60	61	62	63	64	65	66	67
F_n mod 10	0	1	1	2	3	5	8	3	$\cdots$	0	1	1	2	3	5	8	3

To prove that the sequence of last digits of Fibonacci numbers is periodic, consider pairs of remainders modulo m of consecutive Fibonacci numbers:

n	0	1	2	3	4
$\begin{bmatrix} F_n \bmod m \\ F_{n+1} \bmod m \end{bmatrix}$	$\begin{bmatrix} 0 \\ 1 \end{bmatrix}$	$\begin{bmatrix} 1 \\ 1 \end{bmatrix}$	$\begin{bmatrix} 1 \\ 2 \end{bmatrix}$	$\begin{bmatrix} 2 \\ 3 \end{bmatrix}$	$\begin{bmatrix} 3 \\ 5 \end{bmatrix}$

Each column in this table can be computed from the previous column $\begin{bmatrix} a \\ b \end{bmatrix}$ as $\begin{bmatrix} b \\ (a+b) \bmod m \end{bmatrix}$. By the same reasoning, the column *before* the column $\begin{bmatrix} a \\ b \end{bmatrix}$ is $\begin{bmatrix} (b-a) \bmod m \\ a \end{bmatrix}$. Hence, any column in the table above can be extended both to the left and to the right to fill the entire table.

Since, there are only m remainders modulo m, there are only m^2 possible columns. Therefore, some columns will eventually repeat in the table and will be repeated forever:

$$\begin{bmatrix} 0 \\ 1 \end{bmatrix} \quad \cdots \quad \begin{bmatrix} a \\ b \end{bmatrix} \quad \cdots \quad \begin{bmatrix} a \\ b \end{bmatrix} \quad \cdots \quad \begin{bmatrix} a \\ b \end{bmatrix} \quad \cdots \quad \begin{bmatrix} a \\ b \end{bmatrix} \quad \cdots$$

Exercise Break. Prove that the first repeated column in the table for F_n mod m is $\begin{bmatrix} 0 \\ 1 \end{bmatrix}$.

Stop and Think. Why the Pisano period is 60 and not $10^2 = 100$, the number of all possible pairs of remainders modulo 10?

This leads us to the following simple pseudocode for computing the Pisano period modulo m for an arbitrary modulo m.

PISANOPERIOD(m):
$current \leftarrow 0$
$next \leftarrow 1$
$period \leftarrow 0$
while True:
  $oldNext \leftarrow next$
  $next \leftarrow (current + next)$ mod m
  $current \leftarrow oldNext$
  $period \leftarrow period + 1$
  if $current = 0$ and $next = 1$:
    return $period$

One can then check that PISANOPERIOD(10) returns 60. Overall, the pseudocode for the problem looks as follows.

FIBONACCILASTDIGIT(n):
$current \leftarrow 0$
$next \leftarrow 1$
repeat n times:
  $oldNext \leftarrow next$
  $next \leftarrow (current + next)$ mod 10
  $current \leftarrow oldNext$
return $current$

SUMFIBONACCILASTDIGIT(n):
return (FIBONACCILASTDIGIT($(n + 2)$ mod 60) $- 1$) mod 10

```python
# python3


def fibonacci_last_digit(n):
    current, next = 0, 1
    for _ in range(n):
        current, next = next, (current + next) % 10

    return current

if __name__ == '__main__':
    n = int(input())
    print((fibonacci_last_digit((n + 2) % 60) + 9) % 10)
```

Computing the Last Digit of a Fibonacci Number Using Fast Matrix Exponentiation

An alternative way to compute the last digit of a Fibonacci number is to notice that the equations

$$F_n = 0 \cdot F_{n-1} + 1 \cdot F_n$$
$$F_{n+1} = 1 \cdot F_{n-1} + 1 \cdot F_n$$

can be represented as multiplying a 2×2 matrix $\begin{bmatrix} 0 & 1 \\ 1 & 1 \end{bmatrix}$ and a vector $\begin{bmatrix} F_{n-1} \\ F_n \end{bmatrix}$:

$$\begin{bmatrix} F_n \\ F_{n+1} \end{bmatrix} = \begin{bmatrix} 0 & 1 \\ 1 & 1 \end{bmatrix} \cdot \begin{bmatrix} F_{n-1} \\ F_n \end{bmatrix}.$$

Therefore:

$$\begin{bmatrix} F_n \\ F_{n+1} \end{bmatrix} = \begin{bmatrix} 0 & 1 \\ 1 & 1 \end{bmatrix} \cdot \begin{bmatrix} F_{n-1} \\ F_n \end{bmatrix} = \begin{bmatrix} 0 & 1 \\ 1 & 1 \end{bmatrix}^2 \cdot \begin{bmatrix} F_{n-2} \\ F_{n-1} \end{bmatrix} = \cdots = \begin{bmatrix} 0 & 1 \\ 1 & 1 \end{bmatrix}^n \cdot \begin{bmatrix} F_0 \\ F_1 \end{bmatrix}.$$

Hence, F_n is simply the top right element of the n-th power of the matrix $M = \begin{bmatrix} 0 & 1 \\ 1 & 1 \end{bmatrix}$.

Stop and Think. A naive way to compute M^n requires $(n-1)$ matrix multiplications. Can you do it with only $O(\log n)$ matrix multiplications?

We illustrate the idea of the *fast matrix exponentiation* using integers rather than matrices. Given an integer x, a naive way to compute x^9 is to do 8 multiplications. But here is a faster way to compute x^9 with just 4 multiplications:

$$y_1 = x \cdot x,$$
$$y_2 = y_1 \cdot y_1,$$
$$y_3 = y_2 \cdot y_2,$$
$$y_4 = y_3 \cdot x.$$

More generally, if n is even, computing x^n takes just one more multiplication compared to computing $y = x^{n/2}$ since $x^n = x^{n/2} \cdot x^{n/2} = y \cdot y$. If n is odd, computing x^n takes just two more multiplication compared to computing $y = x^{(n-1)/2}$ since $x^n = (x^{(n-1)/2} \cdot x^{(n-1)/2}) \cdot x = y \cdot y \cdot x$.

FastIntegerExponentiation(x, n):
if $n = 0$:
   return 1
if n is even:
   $z \leftarrow$ FastIntegerExponentiation$(x, n/2)$
   return z^2
else:
   $z \leftarrow$ FastIntegerExponentiation$(x, (n-1)/2)$
   return $z^2 \cdot x$

Since each recursive call FastIntegerExponentiation makes two integer multiplications and halves n, it performs at most $2 \log n$ multiplications.

Going back to Fibonacci numbers, recall that F_n is equal to the top right element of M^n. Since we are interested in the last digit of F_n, we simply take every intermediate result modulo 10:

FastMatrixExponentiationModulo10(D, n):
if $n = 0$:
    return the 2×2 identity matrix
if n is even:
    $Z \leftarrow$ FastMatrixExponentiationModulo10($D, n/2$)
    return Multiply2x2MatricesModulo10(Z, Z)
else:
    $Z \leftarrow$ FastMatrixExponentiationModulo10($D, n/2$)
    $Y \leftarrow$ Multiply2x2MatricesModulo10(Z, Z)
    return Multiply2x2MatricesModulo10(Y, D)

Multiply2x2MatricesModulo10(A, B):
$C \leftarrow \begin{bmatrix} 0 & 0 \\ 0 & 0 \end{bmatrix}$
$C_{11} \leftarrow (A_{11} \cdot B_{11} + A_{12} \cdot B_{21}) \bmod 10$
$C_{12} \leftarrow (A_{11} \cdot B_{12} + A_{12} \cdot B_{22}) \bmod 10$
$C_{21} \leftarrow (A_{21} \cdot B_{11} + A_{22} \cdot B_{21}) \bmod 10$
$C_{22} \leftarrow (A_{21} \cdot B_{12} + A_{22} \cdot B_{22}) \bmod 10$
return C

Finally, since $F_0 + F_1 + \cdots + F_n = F_{n+2} - 1$, we compute the $(n+2)$-th power of M.

SumFibonacciLastDigit(n):
$M \leftarrow \begin{bmatrix} 0 & 1 \\ 1 & 1 \end{bmatrix}$
$P \leftarrow$ FastMatrixExponentiationModulo10($M, n + 2$)
return $(P_{21} - 1) \bmod 10$

```python3
# python3


def multiply_2x2_matrices_mod10(A, B):
    C = [[None] * 2 for _ in range(2)]
    C[0][0] = (A[0][0] * B[0][0] + A[0][1] * B[1][0]) % 10
    C[0][1] = (A[0][0] * B[0][1] + A[0][1] * B[1][1]) % 10
    C[1][0] = (A[1][0] * B[0][0] + A[1][1] * B[1][0]) % 10
    C[1][1] = (A[1][0] * B[0][1] + A[1][1] * B[1][1]) % 10
    return C
```

```
def matrix_exponent_mod10(D, n):
    if n == 0:
        return [[1, 0], [0, 1]]
    elif n % 2 == 0:
        Z = matrix_exponent_mod10(D, n // 2)
        return multiply_2x2_matrices_mod10(Z, Z)
    else:
        Z = matrix_exponent_mod10(D, n // 2)
        Y = multiply_2x2_matrices_mod10(Z, Z)
        return multiply_2x2_matrices_mod10(Y, D)


if __name__ == '__main__':
    n = int(input())
    M = [[0, 1], [1, 1]]
    P = matrix_exponent_mod10(M, n + 2)
    print((P[1][0] + 9) % 10)
```

5.7   Last Digit of the Sum of Fibonacci Numbers Again

Last Digit of the Partial Sum of Fibonacci Numbers Problem

Compute the last digit of $F_m + F_{m+1} + \cdots + F_n$.

Input: Integers m and n.

Output: The last digit of $F_m + F_{m+1} + \cdots + F_n$.

$2 + 3 + 5 + 8 + 13 = 31$

Input format. Integers m and n.

Output format. $(F_m + F_{m+1} + \cdots + F_n) \bmod 10$.

Constraints. $0 \le m \le n \le 10^{18}$.

Sample 1.

Input:

3 7

Output:

1

$F_3 + F_4 + F_5 + F_6 + F_7 = 2 + 3 + 5 + 8 + 13 = 31$.

Sample 2.

Input:

10 10

Output:

55

$F_{10} = 55$.

5.8 Last Digit of the Sum of Squares of Fibonacci Numbers

Last Digit of the Sum of Squares of Fibonacci Numbers Problem

Compute the last digit of $F_0^2 + F_1^2 + \cdots + F_n^2$.

Input: Integers n.
Output: The last digit of $F_0^2 + F_1^2 + \cdots + F_n^2$.

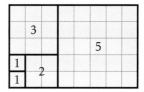

Hint. Since the brute force search algorithm for this problem is too slow (n may be as large as 10^{18}), we need to come up with a simple formula for $F_0^2 + F_1^2 + \cdots + F_n^2$. The figure above represents the sum $F_1^2 + F_2^2 + F_3^2 + F_4^2 + F_5^2$ as the area of a rectangle with vertical side $F_5 = 5$ and horizontal side $F_5 + F_4 = 3 + 5 = F_6$.

Input format. Integer n.

Output format. $F_0^2 + F_1^2 + \cdots + F_n^2 \bmod 10$.

Constraints. $0 \le n \le 10^{18}$.

Sample 1.

    Input:
    7
    Output:
    0

$F_0^2 + F_1^2 + \cdots + F_7^2 = 0 + 1 + 1 + 4 + 9 + 25 + 64 + 169 = 273$.

Sample 2.

Input:

73

Output:

1

$F_0^2 + \cdots + F_{73}^2 = 1\,052\,478\,208\,141\,359\,608\,061\,842\,155\,201$.

Sample 3.

Input:

1234567890

Output:

0

Chapter 6: Greedy Algorithms

In this chapter, you will learn about seemingly naive yet powerful greedy algorithms. After learning the key idea behind the greedy algorithms, some of our students feel that they represent the algorithmic Swiss army knife that can be applied to solve nearly all programming challenges in this book. Be warned: since this intuitive idea rarely works in practice, you have to prove that your greedy algorithm produces an optimal solution! As always, we provide solutions for some problems in this chapter (shown in bold rectangle).

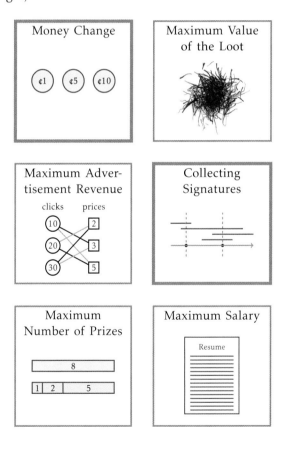

6.1 Money Change

Money Change Problem
Compute the minimum number of coins needed to change the given value into coins with denominations 1, 5, and 10.

> **Input:** Integer *money*.
> **Output:** The minimum number of coins with denominations 1, 5, and 10 that changes *money*.

In this problem, you will implement a simple greedy algorithm used by cashiers all over the world. We assume that a cashier has unlimited number of coins of each denomination.

Input format. Integer *money*.

Output format. The minimum number of coins with denominations 1, 5, 10 that changes *money*.

Constraints. $1 \le money \le 10^3$.

Sample 1.
    Input:
    2
    Output:
    2
    $2 = 1 + 1$.

Sample 2.
    Input:
    28
    Output:
    6
    $28 = 10 + 10 + 5 + 1 + 1 + 1$.

Solution

Here is the idea: while *money* > 0, keep taking a coin with the largest denomination that does not exceed *money*, subtracting its value from *money*, and adding 1 to the count of the number of coins:

```
CHANGEMONEY(money):
numCoins ← 0
while money > 0:
  if money ≥ 10:
    money ← money − 10
  else if money ≥ 5:
    money ← money − 5
  else:
    money ← money − 1
  numCoins ← numCoins + 1
return numCoins
```

There is also a one-liner for solving this problem:

return $\lfloor money/10 \rfloor + \lfloor (money \bmod 10)/5 \rfloor + (money \bmod 5)$

Designing greedy algorithms is easy, but proving that they work is often non-trivial! You are probably wondering why we should waste time proving the correctness of the obvious CHANGEMONEY algorithm. Just wait until we setup an algorithmic trap to convince you that the proof below is not a waste of time!

To prove that this greedy algorithms is correct, we show that taking a coin with the largest denomination is consistent with some optimal solution. I.e., we need to prove that for any positive integer *money* there exists an optimal way of changing *money* that uses at least one coin with denomination D, where D is the largest number among $1, 5, 10$ that does not exceed *money*. We prove this by considering a few cases. In each of the cases we take some solution (i.e., a particular change for *money*) and transform it so that the number of coins does not increase and it contains at least one coin with denomination D. In particular, if we start from an *optimal* way to change *money* what we get is also an *optimal* way of changing *money* that contains a coin D.

1. $1 \le money < 5$. In this case $D = 1$ and the only way to change *money*

is to use *money* coins of denomination 1.

2. $5 \leq money < 10$. In this case $D = 5$. Clearly, any change of *money* uses only coins with denominations 1 and 5. If it does not use a coin with denomination 5, then it uses at least five coins of denomination 1 (since *money* ≥ 5). By replacing them with one coin of denomination 5 we improve this solution.

3. $10 \leq money$. In this case $D = 10$. Consider a way of changing *money* and assume that it does not use a coin 10. A simple, but crucial observation is that some subset of the used coins sums up to 10. This can be shown by considering the number of coins of denomination 5 in this solution: if there are no 5's, then there are at least ten 1's and we replace them with a single 10; if there is exactly one 5, then there are at least five 1's and we replace them with a single 10 again; if there are at least two 5's, they can be again replaced.

Although this proof is long and rather boring, you need a proofseach time you come up with a greedy algorithm! The next Exercise Break hints a more compact way of proving the correctness of the algorithm above.

Exercise Break. Show that *money* mod 5 coins of denomination 1 are needed in any solution and that the rest should be changed with coins of denomination 10 and at most one coin of denomination 5.

Running time. The running time of the first algorithm (with the while loop) is $O(m)$ only, while the second algorithm requires only a few arithmetic operations.

Stop and Think. Does this greedy algorithm work for denominations 1, 4, and 6?

6.2 Maximum Value of the Loot

Maximizing the Value of the Loot Problem
Find the maximal value of items that fit into the backpack.

Input: The capacity of a backpack W as well as the weights $(w_1, \ldots, w_n)$ and per pound prices $(p_1, \ldots, p_n)$ of n different compounds.

Output: The maximum total price of items that fit into the backpack of the given capacity: i.e., the maximum value of $p_1 \cdot u_1 + \cdots + p_n \cdot u_n$ such that $u_1 + \cdots + u_n \le W$ and $0 \le u_i \le w_i$ for all i.

A thief breaks into a spice shop and finds four pounds of saffron, three pounds of vanilla, and five pounds of cinnamon. His backpack fits at most nine pounds, therefore he cannot take everything. Assuming that the prices of saffron, vanilla, and cinnamon are \$5 000, \$200, and \$10 per pound respectively, what is the most valuable loot in this case? If the thief takes u_1 pounds of saffron, u_2 pounds of vanilla, and u_3 pounds of cinnamon, the total price of the loot is $5000 \cdot u_1 + 200 \cdot u_2 + 10 \cdot u_3$. The thief would like to maximize the value of this expression subject to the following constraints: $u_1 \le 4$, $u_2 \le 3$, $u_3 \le 5$, $u_1 + u_2 + u_3 \le 9$.

Input format. The first line of the input contains the number n of compounds and the capacity W of a backpack. The next n lines define the prices and weights of the compounds. The i-th line contains the price per pound p_i and the weight w_i of the i-th compound.

Output format. Output the maximum price of compounds that fit into the backpack.

Constraints. $1 \le n \le 10^3$, $0 \le W \le 2 \cdot 10^6$; $0 \le p_i \le 2 \cdot 10^6$, $0 < w_i \le 2 \cdot 10^6$ for all $1 \le i \le n$. All the numbers are integers.

Bells and whistles. Although the Input to this problem consists of integers, the Output may be non-integer. Therefore, the absolute value of the difference between the answer of your program and the optimal value should be at most 10^{-3}. To ensure this, output your answer with at least four digits after the decimal point (otherwise your answer, while being computed correctly, can turn out to be wrong because of rounding issues).

Sample 1.

Input:

```
3 50
60 20
100 50
120 30
```

Output:

```
180.0000
```

To achieve the value 180, the thief takes the whole first compound and the whole third compound.

Sample 2.

Input:

```
1 10
500 30
```

Output:

```
166.6667
```

The thief should take ten pounds of the only available compound.

6.3 Maximum Advertisement Revenue

Maximum Product of Two Sequences Problem

Find the maximum dot product of two sequences of numbers.

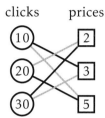

> **Input:** Two sequences of n positive integers: $price_1, \ldots, price_n$ and $clicks_1, \ldots, clicks_n$.
>
> **Output:** The maximum value of $price_1 \cdot c_1 + \cdots + price_n \cdot c_n$, where $c_1, \ldots, c_n$ is a permutation of $clicks_1, \ldots, clicks_n$.

You have $n = 3$ advertisement slots on your popular Internet page and you want to sell them to advertisers. They expect, respectively, $clicks_1 = 10$, $clicks_2 = 20$, and $clicks_3 = 30$ clicks per day. You found three advertisers willing to pay $price_1 = \$2$, $price_2 = \$3$, and $price_3 = \$5$ per click. How would you pair the slots and advertisers? For example, the blue pairing gives a revenue of $10 \cdot 5 + 20 \cdot 2 + 30 \cdot 3 = 180$ dollars, while the black one results in revenue of $10 \cdot 3 + 20 \cdot 5 + 30 \cdot 2 = 190$ dollars.

Input format. The first line contains an integer n, the second one contains a sequence of integers $price_1, \ldots, price_n$, the third one contains a sequence of integers $clicks_1, \ldots, clicks_n$.

Output format. Output the maximum value of $(price_1 \cdot c_1 + \cdots + price_n \cdot c_n)$, where $c_1, \ldots, c_n$ is a permutation of $clicks_1, \ldots, clicks_n$.

Constraints. $1 \le n \le 10^3$; $0 \le price_i, clicks_i \le 10^5$ for all $1 \le i \le n$.

Sample 1.

Input:
```
1
23
39
```
Output:
```
897
```
$897 = 23 \cdot 39$.

Sample 2.

Input:
```
3
2 3 9
7 4 2
```
Output:
```
79
```
$79 = 7 \cdot 9 + 2 \cdot 2 + 3 \cdot 4$.

6.4 Collecting Signatures

Covering Segments by Points Problem
Find the minimum number of points needed to cover all given segments on a line.

Input: A sequence of n segments $[l_1, r_1], \ldots, [l_n, r_n]$ on a line.
Output: A set of points of minimum size such that each segment $[l_i, r_i]$ contains a point, i.e., there exists a point x such that $l_i \le x \le r_i$.

You are responsible for collecting signatures from all tenants in a building. For each tenant, you know a period of time when he or she is at home. You would like to collect all signatures by visiting the building as few times as possible. For simplicity, we assume that when you enter the building, you instantly collect the signatures of all tenants that are in the building at that time.

Input format. The first line of the input contains the number n of segments. Each of the following n lines contains two integers l_i and r_i (separated by a space) defining the coordinates of endpoints of the i-th segment.

Output format. The minimum number k of points on the first line and the integer coordinates of k points (separated by spaces) on the second line. You can output the points in any order. If there are many such sets of points, you can output any set.

Constraints. $1 \le n \le 100$; $0 \le l_i \le r_i \le 10^9$ for all i.

Sample 1.

Input:

```
3
1 3
2 5
3 6
```

Output:

```
1
3
```

All three segments [1,3], [2,5], [3,6] contain the point with coordinate 3.

Sample 2.

Input:

```
4
4 7
1 3
2 5
5 6
```

Output:

```
2
3 6
```

The second and the third segments contain the point with coordinate 3 while the first and the fourth segments contain the point with coordinate 6. All segments cannot be covered by a single point, since the segments [1,3] and [5,6] do not overlap. Another valid solution in this case is the set of points 2 and 5.

Solution

You know the intervals of time $[l_1, r_1], \ldots, [l_n, r_n]$ when n tenants are at home. At what point of time t is it reasonable to visit the building for the *first time*? Clearly, t should be at most $r = \min\{r_1, \ldots, r_n\}$: indeed, if $t > r_i$ for some i, then you don't get a signature of the i-th tenant (you visit the building for the first time when the i-th tenant has already left). Hence, $t \le r$. Also, It is easy to see that it does not make sense to make the first visit before r.

Exercise Break. Prove that if you covered all intervals by making your first visit before r then you can sleep longer and still cover all intervals by postponing your first visit till r. The picture below serves as a hint to this Exercise Break.

After solving the Exercise Break above, you arrive to the following algorithm that arranges the first visit at time r, discard all segments that are covered by r, and iterates:

SEGMENTSCOVER(*segments*):
points ← empty set
while *segments* is not empty:
    r ← minimum right end-point of a segment from *segments*
    add r to *points*
    remove segments covered by r from the set *segments*
return *points*

The running time is $O(n^2)$, where $n = |segments|$, since there are at most n iterations of the while loop (at least one segment is discarded at each iteration) and each iteration boils down to two scans of the list *segments* (one scan to find the value of r and another one to remove segments that are covered by r).

```python3
# python3

from sys import stdin
from collections import namedtuple

Segment = namedtuple('Segment', 'left right')


def is_covered(segment, point):
```

```
      return segment.left <= point <= segment.right


def segments_cover(segments):
    points = list()
    while len(segments) > 0:
        r = min([s.right for s in segments])
        points.append(r)
        segments = [s for s in segments if not is_covered(s, r)]

    return points

if __name__ == '__main__':
    n, *data = map(int, stdin.read().split())
    input_segments = list(map(lambda x: Segment(x[0], x[1]),
                        zip(data[::2], data[1::2])))
    output_points = segments_cover(input_segments)
    print(len(output_points))
    print(" ".join(map(str, output_points)))
```

This algorithm is already sufficiently fast to pass the grader. To reduce the running time from $O(n^2)$ to $O(n \log n)$, you can simply sort segments in increasing order of their right-end points and scan the resulting list just once. An example of the answer computed by this algorithm is shown below.

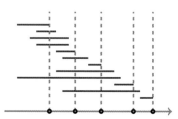

```
# python3


from sys import stdin
from collections import namedtuple

Segment = namedtuple('Segment', 'left right')
```

```python
def segments_cover(segments):
    points = list()
    segments = sorted(segments, key=lambda s: s.right)
    r = -1
    for segment in segments:
        if r < segment.left:
            r = segment.right
            points.append(r)

    return points

if __name__ == '__main__':
    n, *data = map(int, stdin.read().split())
    input_segments = list(map(lambda x: Segment(x[0], x[1]),
                          zip(data[::2], data[1::2])))
    output_points = segments_cover(input_segments)
    print(len(output_points))
    print(" ".join(map(str, output_points)))
```

6.5 Maximum Number of Prizes

Distinct Summands Problem

Represent a positive integer as the sum of the maximum number of pairwise distinct positive integers.

> **Input:** Positive integer n.
>
> **Output:** The maximum k such that n can be represented as the sum $a_1 + \cdots + a_k$ of k distinct integers.

8

1	2	5

You are organizing a competition for children and have n candies to give as prizes. You would like to use these candies for top k places in a competition with a restriction that a higher place gets a larger number of candies. To make as many children happy as possible, you need to find the largest value of k for which it is possible.

Input format. Integer n.

Output format. In the first line, output the maximum number k such that n can be represented as the sum of k pairwise distinct positive integers. In the second line, output k pairwise distinct positive integers that sum up to n (if there are many such representations, output any of them).

Constraints. $1 \le n \le 10^9$.

Sample 1.

> Input:
>
> 6
>
> Output:
>
> 3
>
> 1 2 3

Sample 2.

    Input:

     8

    Output:

     3

     1 2 5

Sample 3.

    Input:

     2

    Output:

     1

     2

6.6   Maximum Salary

Largest Concatenate Problem

Compile the largest number by concatenating the given numbers.

> **Input:** A sequence of positive integers.
>
> **Output:** The largest number that can be obtained by concatenating the given integers in some order.

This is probably the most important problem in this book :). As the last question of an interview, your future boss gives you a few pieces of paper with a single number written on each of them and asks you to compose a largest number from these numbers. The resulting number is going to be your salary, so you are very motivated to solve this problem!

This is a simple greedy algorithm:

LargestConcatenate(*Numbers*):
yourSalary ← empty string
while *Numbers* is not empty:
    maxNumber ← −∞
    for each *number* in *Numbers*:
        if *number* ≥ *maxNumber*:
            maxNumber ← *number*
    append *maxNumber* to *yourSalary*
    remove *maxNumber* from *Numbers*
return *yourSalary*

Unfortunately, this algorithm does not always maximize your salary! For example, for an input consisting of two integers 23 and 3 it returns 233, while the largest number is 323.

Exercise Break. Prove that the algorithm works correctly for the case of single-digit numbers.

Not to worry, all you need to do to maximize your salary is to replace the line

> if *number* ≥ *maxNumber*:

with the following line:

> if IsBetter(*number*, *maxNumber*):

for an appropriately implemented function IsBetter. For example, IsBetter(3, 23) should return True.

Stop and Think. How would you implement IsBetter?

Input format. The first line of the input contains an integer n. The second line contains integers $a_1, \ldots, a_n$.

Output format. The largest number that can be composed out of $a_1, \ldots, a_n$.

Constraints. $1 \leq n \leq 100$; $1 \leq a_i \leq 10^3$ for all $1 \leq i \leq n$.

Sample 1.
> Input:
> 2
> 21 2
> Output:
> 221
> Note that in this case the above algorithm also returns an incorrect answer 212.

Sample 2.
> Input:
> 5
> 9 4 6 1 9
> Output:
> 99641
> The input consists of single-digit numbers only, so the algorithm above returns the correct answer.

Sample 3.

Input:

```
3
23 39 92
```

Output:

```
923923
```

The (incorrect) LARGESTNUMBER algorithm nevertheless produces the correct answer in this case, another reminder to always prove the correctness of your greedy algorithms!

Chapter 7: Divide-and-Conquer

In this chapter, you will learn about divide-and-conquer algorithms that will help you to search huge databases a million times faster than brute-force algorithms. Armed with this algorithmic technique, you will learn in our Coursera and edX MOOCs that the standard way to multiply numbers (that you learned in the grade school) is far from being the fastest! We will then apply the divide-and-conquer technique to design fast sorting algorithms. You will learn that these algorithms are optimal, i.e., even the legendary computer scientist Alan Turing would not be able to design a faster sorting algorithm! We give a solution of one of the problems in this chapter (shown in bold rectangle).

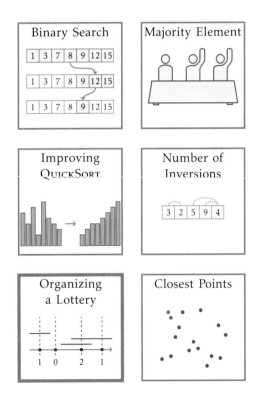

7.1   Binary Search

Before you implement the binary search algorithm, try to solve our *Clock Game* puzzle in which you make repeated guesses of the price of an item, with the computer telling you only whether the true price is higher or lower than the most recent guess. One possible strategy for the Clock Game is to pick a range of prices within which the item's price must fall, and then guess a price halfway between these two extremes. If this guess is incorrect, then you immediately eliminate the half of possible prices. You then make a guess in the middle range of the remaining possible prices, eliminating half of them again. Iterating this strategy quickly yields the price of the item.

This strategy for the Clock Game motivates a *binary search* algorithm for finding the position of an element q within a sorted array K. Before you implement this algorithm, try to solve our Opposite Colors puzzle.

Sorted Array Search Problem
Search a key in a sorted array of keys.

> **Input:**   A sorted array $K = [k_0, \ldots, k_{n-1}]$ of distinct integers (i.e., $k_0 < k_1 < \cdots < k_{n-1}$) and an integer q.
> **Output:** Check whether q occurs in K.

A naive way to solve this problem, is to scan the array K (running time $O(n)$). The BINARYSEARCH algorithm below solves the problem in $O(\log n)$ time. It is initialized by setting *minIndex* equal to 0 and *maxIndex* equal to $n - 1$. It sets *midIndex* to $(minIndex + maxIndex)/2$ and then checks to see whether q is greater than or less than $K[midIndex]$. If q is larger than this value, then BINARYSEARCH iterates on the subarray of K from *minIndex* to *midIndex* $- 1$; otherwise, it iterates on the subarray of K from *midIndex* $+ 1$ to *maxIndex*. Iteration eventually identifies whether q occurs in K.

```
BinarySearch(K[0..n − 1], q)
  minIndex ← 0
  maxIndex ← n − 1
  while maxIndex ≥ minIndex:
    midIndex ← ⌊(minIndex + maxIndex)/2⌋
    if K[midIndex] = q:
      return midIndex
    else if K[midIndex] < q:
      minIndex ← midIndex + 1
    else:
      maxIndex ← midIndex − 1
  return "key not found"
```

For example, if $q = 9$ and $K = [1, 3, 7, 8, 9, 12, 15]$, BinarySearch would first set $minIndex = 0$, $maxIndex = 6$, and $midIndex = 3$. Since q is greater than $K[midIndex] = 8$, we examine the subarray whose elements are greater than $K[midIndex]$ by setting $minIndex = 4$, so that $midIndex$ is recomputed as $(4+6)/2 = 5$. This time, q is smaller than $K[midIndex] = 12$, and so we examine the subarray whose elements are smaller than this value. This subarray consists of a single element, which is q.

The running time of BinarySearch is $O(\log n)$ since it reduces the length of the subarray by at least a factor of 2 at each iteration of the while loop. Note however that our grading system is unable to check whether you implemented a fast $O(\log n)$ algorithm for the Sorted Array Search or a naive $O(n)$ algorithm. The reason is that any program needs a linear time in order to just read the input data. For this reason, we ask you to solve the following more general problem.

Sorted Array Multiple Search Problem

Search multiple keys in a sorted sequence of keys.

> **Input:** A sorted array $K = [k_0, \ldots, k_{n-1}]$ of distinct integers and an array $Q = \{q_0, \ldots, q_{m-1}\}$ of integers.
> **Output:** For each q_i, check whether it occurs in K.

Input format. The first line of the input contains an integer n and a sequence $k_0 < k_1 < \ldots < k_{n-1}$ of n distinct positive integers in increasing order. The next line contains an integer m and m positive integers $q_0, q_1, \ldots, q_{m-1}$.

Output format. For all i from 0 to $m-1$, output an index $0 \le j \le n-1$ such that $k_j = q_i$ or -1, if there is no such index.

Constraints. $1 \le n, m \le 10^4$; $1 \le k_i \le 10^9$ for all $0 \le i < n$; $1 \le q_j \le 10^9$ for all $0 \le j < m$.

Sample.

Input:

```
5 1 5 8 12 13
5 8 1 23 1 11
```

Output:

```
2 0 -1 0 -1
```

Queries 8, 1, and 1 occur at positions 3, 0, and 0, respectively, while queries 23 and 11 do not occur in the sequence of keys.

7.2 Majority Element

Majority Element Problem
Check whether a given sequence of numbers contains an element that appears more than half of the times.

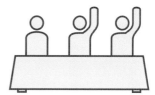

> **Input:** A sequence of n integers.
> **Output:** 1, if there is an element that is repeated more than $n/2$ times, and 0 otherwise.

Here is the naive algorithm for solving the Majority Element Problem with quadratic running time:

MAJORITYELEMENT($A[1..n]$):
for i from 1 to n:
$\quad$ *currentElement* $\leftarrow A[i]$
$\quad$ *count* $\leftarrow 0$
$\quad$ for j from 1 to n:
$\quad\quad$ if $A[j] =$ *currentElement*:
$\quad\quad\quad$ *count* $\leftarrow$ *count* $+ 1$
$\quad$ if *count* $> n/2$:
$\quad\quad$ return *currentElement*
return "no majority element"

Hint. As you might have already guessed, this problem can be solved by the divide-and-conquer algorithm in time $O(n \log n)$. Indeed, if a sequence of length n contains a majority element, then the same element is also a majority element for one of its halves. Thus, to solve this problem you first split a given sequence into halves and recursively solve it for each half. Do you see how to combine the results of two recursive calls?

Exercise Break. Prove that this idea leads to an algorithm with running time $O(n \log n)$.

Input format. The first line contains an integer n, the next one contains a sequence of n non-negative integers $a_1, \ldots, a_n$.

Output format. Output 1 if the sequence contains an element that appears more than $n/2$ times, and 0 otherwise.

Constraints. $1 \le n \le 10^5$; $0 \le a_i \le 10^9$ for all $1 \le i \le n$.

Sample 1.

Input:

5

2 3 9 2 2

Output:

1

2 is the majority element.

Sample 2.

Input:

4

1 2 3 1

Output:

0

This sequence does not have a majority element (note that the element 1 is not a majority element).

Exercise Break. Can you design an even faster $O(n)$ algorithm?

7.3   Improving QUICKSORT

The QUICKSORT algorithm presented in Section 2.7 becomes to be slow in the case when the input array contains many repeated elements. For example, when all elements in the input array are the same, the partition procedure splits the array into two parts, one empty part and the other part with $n-1$ elements. Since QUICKSORT spends $a \cdot n$ time to perform this partition, its overall running time is:

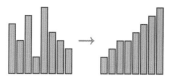

$$a \cdot n + a \cdot (n-1) + a \cdot (n-2) + \ldots = a \cdot \frac{n \cdot (n+1)}{2} .$$

Your goal is to modify the QUICKSORT algorithm so that it works fast even on sequences containing many identical elements.

Input format. The first line of the input contains an integer n. The next line contains a sequence of n integers $a_0, a_1, \ldots, a_{n-1}$.

Output format. Output this sequence sorted in non-decreasing order.

Constraints. $1 \le n \le 10^5$; $1 \le a_i \le 10^9$ for all $0 \le i < n$.

Sample.

Input:
5
2 3 9 2 2
Output:
2 2 2 3 9

7.4 Number of Inversions

Number of Inversions Problem
Compute the number of inversions in a sequence of integers.

> **Input:** A sequence of integers $a_1, \ldots, a_n$.
> **Output:** The number of inversions in the sequence, i.e., the number of indices $i < j$ such that $a_i > a_j$.

The number of inversions in a sequence measures how close the sequence is to being sorted. For example, a sequence sorted in the nondescending order contains no inversions, while a sequence sorted in the descending order contains $n(n-1)/2$ inversions (every two elements form an inversion).

A naive algorithm for the Number of Inversions Problem goes through all possible pairs (i, j) and has running time $O(n^2)$. To solve this problem in time $O(n \log n)$ using the divide-and-conquer technique split the input array into two halves and make a recursive call on both halves. What remains to be done is computing the number of inversions formed by two elements from different halves. If we do this naively, this will bring us back to $O(n^2)$ running time, since the total number of such pairs is $\frac{n}{2} \cdot \frac{n}{2} = \frac{n^2}{4} = O(n^2)$. It turns out that one can compute the number of inversions formed by two elements from different halves in time $O(n)$, if both halves are already sorted. This suggest that instead of solving the original problem we solve a more general problem: compute the number of inversions in the given array and sort it at the same time.

Exercise Break. Modify the MERGESORT algorithm for solving this problem.

Input format. The first line contains an integer n, the next one contains a sequence of integers $a_1, \ldots, a_n$.

Output format. The number of inversions in the sequence.

Constraints. $1 \le n \le 30\,000$, $1 \le a_i \le 10^9$ for all $1 \le i \le n$.

Sample.

Input:

5

2 3 9 2 9

Output:

2

The two inversions here are $(2,4)$ $(a_2 = 3 > 2 = a_4)$ and $(3,4)$ $(a_3 = 9 > 2 = a_4)$.

7.5   Organizing a Lottery

Points and Segments Problem
Given a set of points and a set of segments on a line, compute, for each point, the number of segments it is contained in.

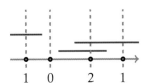

Input: A set of segments and a set of points.
Output: The number of segments containing each point.

You are organizing an online lottery. To participate, a person bets on a single integer. You then draw several segments of consecutive integers at random. A participant's payoff is proportional to the number of segments that contain the participant's number. You need an efficient algorithm for computing the payoffs for all participants. A simple scan of the list of all ranges for each participant is too slow since your lottery is very popular: you have thousands of participants and thousands of ranges.

Input format. The first line contains two non-negative integers n and m defining the number of segments and the number of points on a line, respectively. The next n lines contain two integers l_i, r_i defining the i-th segment $[l_i, r_i]$. The next line contains m integers defining points $p_1, \ldots, p_m$.

Output format. m non-negative integers $k_1, \ldots, k_p$ where k_i is the number of segments that contain p_i.

Constraints. $1 \leq n, m \leq 50\,000$; $-10^8 \leq l_i \leq r_i \leq 10^8$ for all $1 \leq i \leq n$; $-10^8 \leq p_j \leq 10^8$ for all $1 \leq j \leq m$.

Sample 1.

Input:

2 3
0 5
7 10
1 6 11

Output:

1 0 0

We have two segments and three points. The first point lies only in the first segment while the remaining two points are outside of all segments.

Sample 2.

Input:

1 3
−10 10
−100 100 0

Output:

0 0 1

Sample 3.

Input:

3 2
0 5
−3 2
7 10
1 6

Output:

2 0

Solution 1: Sorting All Points

Consider an example with $n = 2$ segments $[l_1, r_1] = [4, 10]$, $[l_2, r_2] = [1, 8]$ and $m = 3$ points $p_1 = 11$, $p_2 = 7$, $p_3 = 3$:

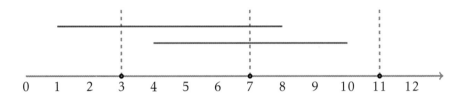

Let's now initialize *numberOfSegments* to 0 and scan the line above from the left to the right. We will increase (decrease) *numberOfSegments* by 1 each time we encounter a left (right) end-point of an interval. Initially, *numberOfSegments* is set to 0. We arrive to $l_2 = 1$ and increment *numberOfSegments*. We then move on to p_3. This is a point from the dataset (rather than an end-point of a segment), so we don't change the value of *numberOfSegments*, but we now know that $p_3 = 3$ is covered by a single segment. We then proceed to l_1 and increment *numberOfSegments* again. We then meet another point p_2. As with the previous point, we know that it is covered by *numberOfSegments* = 2 segments. We move on to r_2 and decrement *numberOfSegments*. We decrement it once again when we reach r_1. Finally, we end our journey at p_2 that is covered by *numberOfSegments* = 0 segments. The value of *numberOfSegments* for each point is shown below.

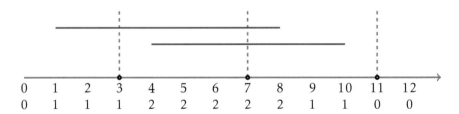

Intuitively, we are moving along a line maintaining the invariant that *numberOfSegments* is equal to the number of segments containing a given point. For a given point, the segments that contain it start to the left of the point and end to the right of the point. And this is exactly what we count. Note that each segment that starts and ends to the left of the point first contributes +1 to *numberOfSegments*, but then cancels this by contributing −1.

The only remaining issue is how to handle coinciding points and segment ends. For example, what if $[l_1, r_1] = [1, 3]$, $p_1 = 3$, and $[l_2, r_2] = [3, 7]$?

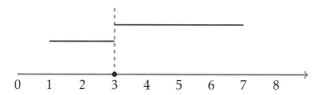

That is, there are three different objects at the point with coordinate 3: the end $r_1 = 3$ of the first segment, the point $p_1 = 3$, and the beginning of the second segment $l_2 = 3$. It is important to process these three events in the following order:

1. We first process l_2 and set *numberOfSegments* to 2.

2. We then report that p_1 is covered by *numberOfSegments* = 2 segments.

3. We then process r_1 and decrement *numberOfSegments*.

In other words, for a given point we need to first process all segments that start at this point, then report the number of segments covering it, and then process all segments that end at this point. To make sure that we process all the events in this order, we use 'l', 'p', and 'r' as indicators for left-ends, points, and right-ends in the code below. The needed order is then guaranteed by the lexicographical ordering of these indicators since $l < p < r$.

```python
# python3
from sys import stdin
from collections import namedtuple

Event = namedtuple('Event', ['coordinate', 'type', 'index'])


def points_cover(starts, ends, points):
    count = [None] * len(points)

    events = []
    for i in range(len(starts)):
        events.append(Event(starts[i], 'l', i))
        events.append(Event(ends[i], 'r', i))
    for i in range(len(points)):
```

```
        events.append(Event(points[i], 'p', i))

    events = sorted(events)
    number_of_segments = 0
    for e in events:
        if e.type == 'l':
            number_of_segments += 1
        elif e.type == 'r':
            number_of_segments -= 1
        elif e.type == 'p':
            count[e.index] = number_of_segments
        else:
            assert False

    return count

if __name__ == '__main__':
    data = list(map(int, stdin.read().split()))
    n, m = data[0], data[1]
    starts, ends = data[2:2 * n + 2:2], data[3:2 * n + 2:2]
    points = data[2 * n + 2:]

    count = points_cover(starts, ends, points)
    print(" ".join(map(str, count)))
```

The running time is $O((n+m)\log(n+m))$ since, as we explain later in this book, an array with k elements can be sorted in $O(k \log k)$ time.

Solution 2: Organizing a Lottery and Binary Search

Let before(p) be the number of segments that start before a point p, after(p) be the number of segments that start after p, and cover(p) be the number of segments covering p.

Exercise Break. Prove that for each point p, before(p)+after(p)+cover(p) is equal to the total number of segments.

Hence, to count the number of segments that do not cover the given point p, it is sufficient to count the number of right-ends of segments that are smaller than p and the number of left-ends of segments that are greater than p. If all left-ends and right-ends are sorted, one can use the binary search algorithm to perform such a check in $O(\log n)$ time. The corresponding solution has running time $O(m \log m + n \log m)$.

```python
# python3
from sys import stdin
from bisect import bisect_left, bisect_right


def points_cover(starts, ends, points):
    starts, ends = sorted(starts), sorted(ends)

    count = [len(starts)] * len(points)
    for index, point in enumerate(points):
        count[index] -= bisect_left(ends, point)
        count[index] -= len(starts) - bisect_right(starts, point)

    return count

if __name__ == '__main__':
    data = list(map(int, stdin.read().split()))
    n, m = data[0], data[1]
    starts, ends = data[2:2 * n + 2:2], data[3:2 * n + 2:2]
    points = data[2 * n + 2:]

    count = points_cover(starts, ends, points)
    print(" ".join(map(str, count)))
```

7.6   Closest Points

Closest Points Problem
Find the closest pair of points in a set of points on a plane.

   Input: A set of points on a planc.
   Output: The minimum distance
   between a pair of these points.

This computational geometry problem has many applications in computer graphics and vision. A naive algorithm with quadratic running time iterates through all pairs of points to find the closest pair. Your goal is to design an $O(n \log n)$ time divide and conquer algorithm.

To solve this problem in time $O(n \log n)$, let's first split the given n points by an appropriately chosen vertical line into two halves S_1 and S_2 of size $\frac{n}{2}$ (assume for simplicity that all x-coordinates of the input points are different). By making two recursive calls for the sets S_1 and S_2, we find the minimum distances d_1 and d_2 in these subsets. Let $d = \min\{d_1, d_2\}$.

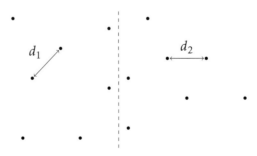

It remains to check whether there exist points $p_1 \in S_1$ and $p_2 \in S_2$ such that the distance between them is smaller than d. We cannot afford to check all possible such pairs since there are $\frac{n}{2} \cdot \frac{n}{2} = \Theta(n^2)$ of them. To check this faster, we first discard all points from S_1 and S_2 whose x-distance to the middle line is greater than d. That is, we focus on the following strip:

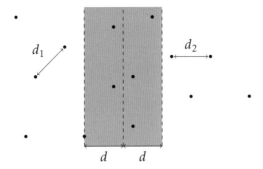

Stop and Think. Why can we narrow the search to this strip?

Now, let's sort the points of the strip by their y-coordinates and denote the resulting sorted list by $P = [p_1, \ldots, p_k]$. It turns out that if $|i - j| > 7$, then the distance between points p_i and p_j is greater than d for sure. This follows from the Exercise Break below.

Exercise Break. Partition the strip into $d \times d$ squares as shown below and show that each such square contains at most four input points.

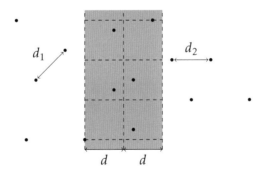

This results in the following algorithm. We first sort the given n points by their x-coordinates and then split the resulting sorted list into two halves S_1 and S_2 of size $\frac{n}{2}$. By making a recursive call for each of the sets S_1 and S_2, we find the minimum distances d_1 and d_2 in them. Let $d = \min\{d_1, d_2\}$. However, we are not done yet as we also need to find the minimum distance between points from different sets (i.e, a point from S_1 and a point from S_2) and check whether it is smaller than d. To perform such a check, we filter the initial point set and keep only those points whose x-distance to the middle line does not exceed d. Afterwards, we sort the set of points in the resulting strip by their y-coordinates and scan the resulting list of points. For each point, we compute its distance to the seven subsequent points in this list and compute d', the minimum distance that we encountered during this scan. Afterwards, we return $\min\{d, d'\}$.

The running time of the algorithm satisfies the recurrence relation

$$T(n) = 2 \cdot T\left(\frac{n}{2}\right) + O(n \log n).$$

The $O(n \log n)$ term comes from sorting the points in the strip by their y-coordinates at every iteration.

Exercise Break. Prove that $T(n) = O(n \log^2 n)$ by analyzing the recursion tree of the algorithm.

Exercise Break. Show how to bring the running time down to $O(n \log n)$ by avoiding sorting at each recursive call.

Input format. The first line contains the number of points n. Each of the following n lines defines a point (x_i, y_i).

Output format. The minimum distance. Recall that the distance between points (x_1, y_1) and (x_2, y_2) is equal to $\sqrt{(x_1 - x_2)^2 + (y_1 - y_2)^2}$. Thus, while the Input contains only integers, the Output is not necessarily integer and you have to pay attention to precision when you report it. The absolute value of the difference between the answer of your program and the optimal value should be at most 10^{-3}. To ensure this, output your answer with at least four digits after the decimal point (otherwise even correctly computed answer may fail to pass our grader because of the rounding errors).

Constraints. $2 \le n \le 10^5$; $-10^9 \le x_i, y_i \le 10^9$ are integers.

Sample 1.

    Input:

    2

    0 0

    3 4

    Output:

    5.0

    There are only two points at distance 5.

Sample 2.

    Input:

    11

    4 4

    -2 -2

    -3 -4

    -1 3

    2 3

    -4 0

    1 1

    -1 -1

    3 -1

    -4 2

    -2 4

    Output:

    1.414213

The smallest distance is $\sqrt{2}$. There are two pairs of points at this distance shown in blue and red below: $(-1,-1)$ and $(-2,-2)$; $(-2,4)$ and $(-1,3)$.

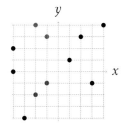

Chapter 8: Dynamic Programming

In this chapter, you will implement various dynamic programming algorithms and will see how they solve problems that evaded all attempts to solve them using greedy or divide-and-conquer strategies. There are countless applications of dynamic programming in practice ranging from searching for similar Internet pages to gene prediction in DNA sequences. You will learn how the same idea helps to automatically make spelling corrections and to find the differences between two versions of the same text.

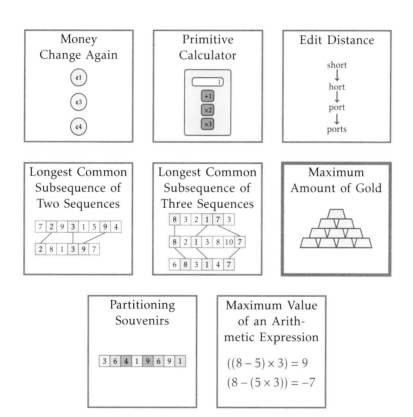

8.1   Money Change Again

As we already know, a natural greedy strategy for the change problem does not work
correctly for any set of denominations. For
example, if the available denominations are
1, 3, and 4, the greedy algorithm will change
6 cents using three coins $(4 + 1 + 1)$ while
it can be changed using just two coins $(3+3)$.
Your goal now is to apply dynamic programming for solving the Money Change
Problem for denominations 1, 3, and 4.

Input format. Integer *money*.

Output format. The minimum number of coins with denominations
    1, 3, 4 that changes *money*.

Constraints. $1 \leq money \leq 10^3$.

Sample 1.

   Input:

   2

   Output:

   2

   $2 = 1 + 1$.

Sample 2.

   Input:

   34

   Output:

   9

   $34 = 3 + 3 + 4 + 4 + 4 + 4 + 4 + 4 + 4$.

8.2 Primitive Calculator

Primitive Calculator Problem

Find the minimum number of operations needed to get a positive integer n from 1 using only three operations: add 1, multiply by 2, and multiply by 3.

> **Input:** An integer *n*.
> **Output:** The minimum number of operations "+1", "×2", and "×3" needed to get *n* from 1.

You are given a calculator that only performs the following three operations with an integer *x*: add 1 to *x*, multiply *x* by 2, or multiply *x* by 3. Given a positive integer *n*, your goal is to find the minimum number of operations needed to obtain *n* starting from the number 1. Before solving the programming challenge below, test your intuition with our Primitive Calculator puzzle.

Let's try a greedy strategy for solving this problem: if the current number is at most $n/3$, multiply it by 3; if it is larger than $n/3$, but at most $n/2$, multiply it by 2; otherwise add 1 to it. This results in the following pseudocode.

```
GreedyCalculator(n):
  numOperations ← 0
  currentNumber ← 1
  while currentNumber < n:
    if currentNumber ≤ n/3:
      currentNumber ← 3 × currentNumber
    else if currentNumber ≤ n/2:
      currentNumber ← 2 × currentNumber
    else:
      currentNumber ← 1 + currentNumber
    numOperations ← numOperations + 1
  return numOperations
```

Stop and Think. Can you find a number n such that
GREEDYCALCULATOR(n) produces an incorrect result?

Input format. An integer n.

Output format. In the first line, output the minimum number k of operations needed to get n from 1. In the second line, output a sequence of intermediate numbers. That is, the second line should contain positive integers $a_0, a_1, \ldots, a_k$ such that $a_0 = 1$, $a_k = n$ and for all $1 \le i \le k$, a_i is equal to either $a_{i-1} + 1$, $2a_{i-1}$, or $3a_{i-1}$. If there are many such sequences, output any one of them.

Constraints. $1 \le n \le 10^6$.

Sample 1.

Input:

```
1
```

Output:

```
0
1
```

Sample 2.

Input:

```
96234
```

Output:

```
14
1 3 9 10 11 22 66 198 594 1782 5346 16038 16039 32078 96234
```

Another valid output in this case is "1 3 9 10 11 33 99 297 891 2673 8019 16038 16039 48117 96234".

8.3   Edit Distance

Edit Distance Problem
Compute the edit distance between two strings.

> **Input:** Two strings.
> **Output:** The minimum number of single symbol insertions, deletions, and substitutions to transform one string into the other one.

Edit distance has many applications in computational biology, natural language processing, spell checking, etc. For example, biologists often analyze edit distances when they search for disease-causing mutations.

Input format. Two strings consisting of lower case latin letters, each on a separate line.

Output format. The edit distance between them.

Constraints. The length of both strings is at least 1 and at most 100.

Sample 1.
> Input:
> short
> ports
>
> Output:
> 3

The second string can be obtained from the first one by deleting s, substituting h for p, and inserting s. This can be compactly visualized by the following *alignment*.

s	h	o	r	t	–
–	p	o	r	t	s

Sample 2.

Input:
```
editing
distance
```

Output:
```
5
```

Delete e, insert s after i, substitute i for a, substitute g for c, insert e to the end.

e	d	i	–	t	i	n	g	–
–	d	i	s	t	a	n	c	e

Sample 3.

Input:
```
ab
ab
```

Output:
```
0
```

8.4 Longest Common Subsequence of Two Sequences

Longest Common Subsequence of Two Sequences Problem
Compute the longest common subsequence of two sequences.

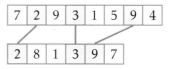

    Input: Two sequences.
    Output: Their longest common subsequence.

Given two sequences $A = (a_1, a_2, \ldots, a_n)$ and $B = (b_1, b_2, \ldots, b_m)$, find the length of their longest common subsequence, i.e., the largest non-negative integer p such that there exist indices

$$1 \le i_1 < i_2 < \cdots < i_p \le n,$$
$$1 \le j_1 < j_2 < \cdots < j_p \le m.$$

such that

$$a_{i_1} = b_{j_1},$$
$$a_{i_2} = b_{j_2},$$
$$\vdots$$
$$a_{i_p} = b_{j_p}.$$

The problem has applications in data comparison (e.g., diff utility, merge operation in various version control systems), bioinformatics (finding similarities between genes in various species), and others.

Input format. First line: n. Second line: $a_1, a_2, \ldots, a_n$. Third line: m. Fourth line: $b_1, b_2, \ldots, b_m$.

Output format. p.

Constraints. $1 \le n, m \le 100$; $-10^9 \le a_i, b_i \le 10^9$ for all i.

Sample 1.

Input:

```
3
2 7 5
2
2 5
```

Output:

```
2
```

A common subsequence of length 2 is $(2, 5)$.

Sample 2.

Input:

```
1
7
4
1 2 3 4
```

Output:

```
0
```

The two sequences do not share elements.

Sample 3.

Input:

```
4
2 7 8 3
4
5 2 8 7
```

Output:

```
2
```

One common subsequence is $(2, 7)$. Another one is $(2, 8)$.

8.5 Longest Common Subsequence of Three Sequences

Longest Common Subsequence of Three Sequences Problem
Compute the longest common subsequence of three sequences.

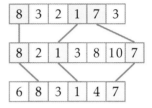

> **Input:** Three sequences.
> **Output:** Their longest common subsequence.

Given three sequences $A = (a_1, a_2, \ldots, a_n)$, $B = (b_1, b_2, \ldots, b_m)$, and $C = (c_1, c_2, \ldots, c_l)$, find the length of their longest common subsequence, i.e., the largest non-negative integer p such that there exist indices

$$1 \le i_1 < i_2 < \cdots < i_p \le n,$$
$$1 \le j_1 < j_2 < \cdots < j_p \le m,$$
$$1 \le k_1 < k_2 < \cdots < k_p \le l$$

such that

$$a_{i_1} = b_{j_1} = c_{k_1},$$
$$a_{i_2} = b_{j_2} = c_{k_2},$$
$$\vdots$$
$$a_{i_p} = b_{j_p} = c_{k_p}.$$

Input format. First line: n. Second line: $a_1, a_2, \ldots, a_n$. Third line: m. Fourth line: $b_1, b_2, \ldots, b_m$. Fifth line: l. Sixth line: $c_1, c_2, \ldots, c_l$.

Output format. p.

Constraints. $1 \le n, m, l \le 100$; $-10^9 \le a_i, b_i, c_i \le 10^9$.

Sample 1.

Input:

```
3
1 2 3
3
2 1 3
3
1 3 5
```

Output:

```
2
```

A common subsequence of length 2 is $(1, 3)$.

Sample 2.

Input:

```
5
8 3 2 1 7
7
8 2 1 3 8 10 7
6
6 8 3 1 4 7
```

Output:

```
3
```

One common subsequence of length 3 in this case is $(8, 3, 7)$. Another one is $(8, 1, 7)$.

8.6   Maximum Amount of Gold

Maximum Amount of Gold Problem
Given a set of gold bars of various weights and a backpack that can hold at most W pounds, place as much gold as possible into the backpack.

> **Input:**   A set of n gold bars of integer weights $w_1, \ldots, w_n$ and a backpack that can hold at most W pounds.
> **Output:** Find a subset of gold bars of maximum total weight not exceeding W.

You found a set of gold bars and your goal is to pack as much gold as possible into your backpack that has capacity W, i.e., it may hold at most W pounds. There is just one copy of each bar and for each bar you can either take it or not (you cannot take a fraction of a bar). Although all bars appear to be identical in the figure above, their weights vary as illustrated in the figure below.

A natural greedy strategy is to grab the heaviest bar that still fits into the remaining capacity of the backpack and iterate. For the set of bars shown above and a backpack of capacity 20, the greedy algorithm would select gold bars of weights 10 and 9. But an optimal solution, containing bars of weights 4, 6, and 10, has a larger weight!

Input format. The first line of the input contains an integer W (capacity of the backpack) and the number n of gold bars. The next line contains n integers $w_1, \ldots, w_n$ defining the weights of the gold bars.

Output format. The maximum weight of gold bars that fits into a backpack of capacity W.

Constraints. $1 \le W \le 10^4$; $1 \le n \le 300$; $0 \le w_1, \ldots, w_n \le 10^5$.

Sample.

Input:

10 3

1 4 8

Output:

9

The sum of the weights of the first and the last bar is equal to 9.

Solution 1: Analyzing the Structure of a Solution

Instead of solving the original problem, we will check whether it is possible to fully pack our backpack with the gold bars: given n gold bars of weights $w_0, \ldots, w_{n-1}$ (we switched to the 0-based indexing) and an integer W, is it possible to select a subset of them of the total weight W?

Exercise Break. Show how to use the solutions to this problem to solve the Maximum Amount of Gold Problem.

Assume that it is possible to fully pack the backpack: there exists a set $S \subseteq \{w_0, \ldots, w_{n-1}\}$ of total weight W. Does it include the last bar of weight w_{n-1}?

Case 1: If $w_{n-1} \notin S$, then a backpack of capacity W can be fully packed using the first $n-1$ bars.

Case 2: If $w_{n-1} \in S$, then we can remove the bar of weight w_{n-1} from the backpack and the remaining bars will have weight $W - w_{n-1}$. Therefore, a backpack of capacity $W - w_{n-1}$ can be fully packed with the first $n-1$ gold bars.

In both cases, we reduced the problem to essentially the same problem with smaller number of items and possibly smaller backpack capacity. We thus consider the variable $pack(w, i)$ equal to true if it is possible to fully pack a backpack of capacity w using the first i bars, and false, otherwise. The analysis of the two cases above leads to the following recurrence relation for $i > 0$,

$$pack(w, i) = pack(w, i - 1) \text{ or } pack(w - w_{i-1}, i - 1).$$

Note that the second term in the above formula does not make sense when $w_{i-1} > w$. Also, $pack(0,0) = \text{true}$, and $pack(0,w) = \text{false}$ for any $w > 0$. Overall,

$$pack(w,i) = \begin{cases} \text{true} & \text{if } i = 0 \text{ and } w = 0 \\ \text{false} & \text{if } i = 0 \text{ and } w > 0 \\ pack(w, i-1) & \text{if } i > 0 \text{ and } w_{i-1} > w \\ pack(w, i-1) \text{ or } pack(w - w_{i-1}, i-1) & \text{otherwise} \end{cases}$$

As i ranges from 0 to n and w ranges from 0 to W, we have $O(nW)$ variables. Since $pack(\cdot, i)$ depends on $pack(\cdot, i-1)$, we process all variables in the increasing order of i. In the pseudocode below, we use a two-dimensional array $pack$ of size $(W+1) \times (n+1)$: $pack[w][i]$ stores the value of $pack(w,i)$. The running time of this solution is $O(nW)$.

KNAPSACK($[w_0, \ldots, w_{n-1}], W$):
$pack \leftarrow$ two-dimensional array of size $(W+1) \times (n+1)$
initialize all elements of $pack$ to false
$pack[0][0] \leftarrow$ true
for i from 1 to n:
  for w from 0 to W:
    if $w_{i-1} > w$:
      $pack[w][i] \leftarrow pack[w][i-1]$
    else:
      $pack[w][i] \leftarrow pack[w][i-1]$ OR $pack[w - w_{i-1}][i-1]$
return $pack[W][n]$

The two-dimensional table below presents the results of the call to KNAPSACK($[1, 3, 4], 8$) and uses F and T to denote false and true values.

	0	1	2	3
0	T	T	T	T
1	F	T	T	T
2	F	F	F	F
3	F	F	T	T
4	F	F	T	T
5	F	F	F	T
6	F	F	F	F
7	F	F	F	T
8	F	F	F	T

```python
# python3
from sys import stdin


def knapsack(weights, capacity):
    n = len(weights)
    pack = [[False] * (n + 1) for _ in range(capacity + 1)]
    pack[0][0] = True

    for i in range(1, n + 1):
        for w in range(capacity + 1):
            if weights[i - 1] > w:
                pack[w][i] = pack[w][i - 1]
            else:
                pack[w][i] = pack[w][i - 1] or \
                             pack[w - weights[i - 1]][i - 1]

    return pack[capacity][n]

if __name__ == '__main__':
    input_capacity, input_n, *input_weights = \
        list(map(int, stdin.read().split()))
    assert len(input_weights) == input_n
    print(knapsack(input_weights, input_capacity))
```

Solution 2: Analyzing All Subsets of Bars

Our goal is to find a subset of n bars of total weight W. A straightforward approach to this problem is to go through all subsets and check whether the weight of one of them is equal to W. Since each bar can be either skipped or taken, each subset of three bars that we analyzed in the previous section ($w_0 = 1$, $w_1 = 3$, $w_2 = 4$) can be represented by a blue-red binary vector:

subset	vector	weight
	000	0
1	100	1
3	010	3
1 3	110	4
4	001	4
1 4	101	5
3 4	011	7
1 3 4	111	8

We will now represent each subset of bars as a path starting at node $(0,0)$ of a $(n+1) \times (W+1)$ grid. If the first bit is blue, it corresponds to a blue horizontal segment in the grid connecting $(0,0)$ with $(0,1)$. If the first bit is red, it corresponds to a red segment in the grid connecting $(0,0)$ with $(1,w_0)$. After processing the first i bits, we will have a blue-red path from $(0,0)$ to some node (i,w) of the grid. If the next bit is blue, we will connect (i,w) with $(i+1,w)$. If the next bit is red, we will connect (i,w) with $(i+1,w+w_i)$ as shown below for the vector 101:

The Figure below shows the paths corresponding to all eight binary vectors of length 3.

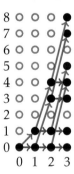

We now superimpose all these eight paths on a single grid:

We classify a node (i, w) in the grid as true if there is a path from $(0,0)$ to (i, w) in the Figure above, and false otherwise. We can fully pack a knapsack of capacity w by a subset of the first i bars if the node (i, w) is true. A node is true if there is either a blue edge or a red edge into this node, i.e., if either $(i-1, w)$ or $(i-1, w-w_{i-1})$ are true. This observation brings us to the previous recurrence relation and the same dynamic programming solution.

Solution 3: Memoization

The following pseudocode recursively computes the recurrence relation from the Solution 1:

RecursiveKnapsack($[w_0, \ldots, w_{n-1}], w, i$):
if $i = 0$ and $w = 0$:
  return true
else if $i = 0$ and $w > 0$:
  return false
else if $i > 0$ and $w_{i-1} > w$:
  return RecursiveKnapsack($[w_0, \ldots, w_{n-1}], w, i - 1$)
else:
  return RecursiveKnapsack($[w_0, \ldots, w_{n-1}], w, i - 1$) OR
      RecursiveKnapsack($[w_0, \ldots, w_{n-1}], w - w_{i-1}, i - 1$)

A call to RecursiveKnapsack($[w_0, \ldots, w_{n-1}], W, n$) solves the problem but is too slow since it recomputes the same values over and over again. To illustrate this, consider a bag of capacity $W = 4$ and $n = 3$ bars of weights $w_0 = 1$, $w_2 = 1$, $w_3 = 1$. A call RecursiveKnapsack($[1, 1, 1], 4, 3$) gives rise to the recursion tree shown below (each node shows the values of (w, i)). Even for this toy example, the value for $(w, i) = (3, 1)$ is computed twice. For 20 bars, the recursive tree may become gigantic with the same value computing millions of times.

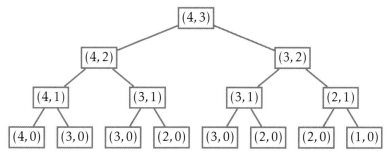

In order to avoid this recursive explosion, we "wrap" our code with *memoization* using an associative array *pack* which is initially empty. An associative array is an abstract data type that stores (*key, value*) pairs. It is supported by many programming languages and is usually implemented as a hash table or a search tree (in C++ and Java it is called a *map*, in Python it is called a *dictionary*). In the implementation below, an associative array *pack* is used to store the Boolean values for (w, i) pairs.

MEMOIZEDKNAPSACK($[w_0, \ldots, w_{n-1}], pack, w, i$):
if (w, i) is not in *pack*:
  if $i = 0$ and $w = 0$:
    $pack[(w,i)] \leftarrow$ true
  else if $i = 0$ and $w > 0$:
    $pack[(w,i)] \leftarrow$ false
  else if $i > 0$ and $w_{i-1} > w$:
    $pack[(w,i)] \leftarrow$ MEMOIZEDKNAPSACK($[w_0, \ldots, w_{n-1}], pack, w, i - 1$)
  else:
    $pack[(w,i)] \leftarrow$ MEMOIZEDKNAPSACK($[w_0, \ldots, w_{n-1}], pack, w, i - 1$) OR
               MEMOIZEDKNAPSACK($[w_0, \ldots, w_{n-1}], pack, w - w_{i-1}, i - 1$)
return $pack[(w,i)]$

The running time of the resulting solution is $O(nW)$ since there are at most that many recursive calls that are not just lookups in the associative array. Thus, the running time is the same as of the corresponding iterative algorithm. In practice, iterative solution are usually faster since they have no recursion overhead and use simpler data structures (e.g., an array instead of a hash table). For the *considered problem*, however, the situation is different: for *some* datasets, the recursive version is faster than the iterative one. For example, if we multiply all the weights by 10, then the running time of the iterative algorithm is also multiplied by 10 while the running time of the recursive algorithms stays essentially the same. In general, if all possible subproblems need to be solved, then the iterative version is usually faster.

```
# python3
from sys import stdin


def memoized(weights, pack, w, i):
    if (w, i) not in pack:
        if i == 0 and w == 0:
            pack[(w, i)] = True
        elif i == 0 and w > 0:
            pack[(w, i)] = False
        elif i > 0 and weights[i - 1] > w:
            pack[(w, i)] = memoized(weights, pack, w, i - 1)
        else:
            pack[(w, i)] = memoized(weights, pack, w, i - 1) or \
                        memoized(weights, pack,
                                 w - weights[i - 1], i - 1)

    return pack[(w, i)]

if __name__ == '__main__':
    input_capacity, input_n, *input_weights = \
        list(map(int, stdin.read().split()))
    assert len(input_weights) == input_n
    print(memoized(input_weights, {}, input_capacity, input_n))
```

8.7   Partitioning Souvenirs

3-Partition Problem
*Partition a set of integers into three subsets with
equal sums.*

Input: Integers $v_1, v_2, \ldots, v_n$.
Output: Check whether it is
possible to partition them into
three subsets with equal sums, i.e.,
check whether there exist three
disjoint sets $S_1, S_2, S_3 \subseteq \{1, 2, \ldots, n\}$
such that $S_1 \cup S_2 \cup S_3 = \{1, 2, \ldots, n\}$
and

$$\sum_{i \in S_1} v_i = \sum_{j \in S_2} v_j = \sum_{k \in S_3} v_k.$$

You and two of your friends have just returned back home after visiting
various countries. Now you would like to evenly split all the souvenirs
that all three of you bought.

Input format. The first line contains an integer n. The second line contains integers $v_1, v_2, \ldots, v_n$ separated by spaces.

Output format. Output 1, if it possible to partition $v_1, v_2, \ldots, v_n$ into three
subsets with equal sums, and 0 otherwise.

Constraints. $1 \le n \le 20$, $1 \le v_i \le 30$ for all i.

Sample 1.
   Input:
   4
   3 3 3 3
   Output:
   0

Sample 2.

Input:

1

30

Output:

0

Sample 3.

Input:

13

1 2 3 4 5 5 7 7 8 10 12 19 25

Output:

1

$1 + 3 + 7 + 25 = 2 + 4 + 5 + 7 + 8 + 10 = 5 + 12 + 19$.

8.8   Maximum Value of an Arithmetic Expression

Maximum Value of an Arithmetic Expression Problem

Parenthesize an arithmetic expression to maximize its value.

Input: An arithmetic expression consisting of digits as well as plus, minus, and multiplication signs.
Output: Add parentheses to the expression in order to maximize its value.

$$((8-5) \times 3) = 9$$
$$(8 - (5 \times 3)) = -7$$

For example, for an expression $(3 + 2 \times 4)$ there are two ways of parenthesizing it: $(3 + (2 \times 4)) = 11$ and $((3 + 2) \times 4) = 20$.

Exercise Break. Parenthesize the expression "$(5 - 8 + 7 \times 4 - 8 + 9)$" to maximize its value.

Input format. The only line of the input contains a string s of length $2n + 1$ for some n, with symbols $s_0, s_1, \ldots, s_{2n}$. Each symbol at an even position of s is a digit (that is, an integer from 0 to 9) while each symbol at an odd position is one of three operations from $\{+, -, *\}$.

Output format. The maximum possible value of the given arithmetic expression among all possible orders of applying arithmetic operations.

Constraints. $1 \leq n \leq 14$ (hence the string contains at most 29 symbols).

Sample.

Input:
```
5-8+7*4-8+9
```
Output:
```
200
```
$$200 = (5 - ((8 + 7) \times (4 - (8 + 9))))$$

Appendix

Compiler Flags

C (gcc 5.2.1). File extensions: .c. Flags:

```
gcc -pipe -O2 -std=c11 <filename> -lm
```

C++ (g++ 5.2.1). File extensions: .cc, .cpp. Flags:

```
g++ -pipe -O2 -std=c++14 <filename> -lm
```

If your C/C++ compiler does not recognize -std=c++14 flag, try replacing it with -std=c++0x flag or compiling without this flag at all (all starter solutions can be compiled without it). On Linux and MacOS, you most probably have the required compiler. On Windows, you may use your favorite compiler or install, e.g., cygwin.

C# (mono 3.2.8). File extensions: .cs. Flags:

```
mcs
```

Haskell (ghc 7.8.4). File extensions: .hs. Flags:

```
ghc -O2
```

Java (Open JDK 8). File extensions: .java. Flags:

```
javac -encoding UTF-8
java -Xmx1024m
```

JavaScript (Node v6.3.0). File extensions: .js. Flags:

```
nodejs
```

Python 2 (CPython 2.7). File extensions: .py2 or .py (a file ending in .py needs to have a first line which is a comment containing "python2"). No flags:

```
python2
```

Python 3 (CPython 3.4). File extensions: .py3 or .py (a file ending in .py needs to have a first line which is a comment containing "python3"). No flags:

```
python3
```

Ruby (Ruby 2.1.5). File extensions: .rb.

```
ruby
```

Scala (Scala 2.11.6). File extensions: .scala.

```
scalac
```

Frequently Asked Questions

What Are the Possible Grading Outcomes?

There are only two outcomes: "pass" or "no pass." To pass, your program must return a correct answer on all the test cases we prepared for you, and do so under the time and memory constraints specified in the problem statement. If your solution passes, you get the corresponding feedback "Good job!" and get a point for the problem. Your solution fails if it either crashes, returns an incorrect answer, works for too long, or uses too much memory for some test case. The feedback will contain the index of the first test case on which your solution failed and the total number of test cases in the system. The tests for the problem are numbered from 1 to the total number of test cases for the problem, and the program is always tested on all the tests in the order from the first test to the test with the largest number.

Here are the possible outcomes:

- Good job! Hurrah! Your solution passed, and you get a point!

- Wrong answer. Your solution outputs incorrect answer for some test case. Check that you consider all the cases correctly, avoid integer overflow, output the required white spaces, output the floating point numbers with the required precision, don't output anything in addition to what you are asked to output in the output specification of the problem statement.

- `Time limit exceeded.` Your solution worked longer than the allowed time limit for some test case. Check again the running time of your implementation. Test your program locally on the test of maximum size specified in the problem statement and check how long it works. Check that your program doesn't wait for some input from the user which makes it to wait forever.

- `Memory limit exceeded.` Your solution used more than the allowed memory limit for some test case. Estimate the amount of memory that your program is going to use in the worst case and check that it does not exceed the memory limit. Check that your data structures fit into the memory limit. Check that you don't create large arrays or lists or vectors consisting of empty arrays or empty strings, since those in some cases still eat up memory. Test your program locally on the tests of maximum size specified in the problem statement and look at its memory consumption in the system.

- `Cannot check answer. Perhaps the output format is wrong.` This happens when you output something different than expected. For example, when you are required to output either "Yes" or "No", but instead output 1 or 0. Or your program has empty output. Or your program outputs not only the correct answer, but also some additional information (please follow the exact output format specified in the problem statement). Maybe your program doesn't output anything, because it crashes.

- `Unknown signal 6 (or 7, or 8, or 11, or some other).` This happens when your program crashes. It can be because of a division by zero, accessing memory outside of the array bounds, using uninitialized variables, overly deep recursion that triggers a stack overflow, sorting with a contradictory comparator, removing elements from an empty data structure, trying to allocate too much memory, and many other reasons. Look at your code and think about all those possibilities. Make sure that you use the same compiler and the same compiler flags as we do.

- `Internal error: exception...` Most probably, you submitted a compiled program instead of a source code.

- Grading failed. Something wrong happened with the system. Report this through Coursera or edX Help Center.

Why the Test Cases Are Hidden?

See section 3.2.4.

May I Post My Solution at the Forum?

Please do not post any solutions at the forum or anywhere on the web, even if a solution does not pass the tests (as in this case you are still revealing parts of a correct solution). Our students follow the Honor Code: "I will not make solutions to homework, quizzes, exams, projects, and other assignments available to anyone else (except to the extent an assignment explicitly permits sharing solutions)."

Do I Learn by Trying to Fix My Solution?

My implementation always fails in the grader, though I already tested and stress tested it a lot. Would not it be better if you gave me a solution to this problem or at least the test cases that you use? I will then be able to fix my code and will learn how to avoid making mistakes. Otherwise, I do not feel that I learn anything from solving this problem. I am just stuck.

First of all, learning from your mistakes is one of the best ways to learn.

The process of trying to invent new test cases that might fail your program is difficult but is often enlightening. Thinking about properties of your program makes you understand what happens inside your program and in the general algorithm you're studying much more.

Also, it is important to be able to find a bug in your implementation without knowing a test case and without having a reference solution, just like in real life. Assume that you designed an application and an annoyed user reports that it crashed. Most probably, the user will not tell you the exact sequence of operations that led to a crash. Moreover, there will be no reference application. Hence, it is important to learn how to find a bug in your implementation yourself, without a magic oracle giving you either a test case that your program fails or a reference solution. We encourage you to use programming assignments in this class as a way of practicing this important skill.

If you have already tested your program on all corner cases you can imagine, constructed a set of manual test cases, applied stress testing, etc, but your program still fails, try to ask for help on the forum. We encourage you to do this by first explaining what kind of corner cases you have already considered (it may happen that by writing such a post you will realize that you missed some corner cases!), and only afterwards asking other learners to give you more ideas for tests cases.